I0008488

Trusted by Design, Exposed by Convergence

Legacy OT in a Converged World: The Unraveling of Designed Trust

Bill Johns
Peninsula Network Security, LLC
2025

Disclaimer:

Information about the attribution of cyberattacks and details of proprietary protocols are often not disclosed in detail, or at all. Due to this, attribution, methods of attack, undisclosed protocol features, and other similar details are often reported variously by a variety of sources including news releases, cyber security analysts, and others – and thus, they may not be entirely accurate. This is the nature of the world that these events take place in.

DEDICATION

To my peers in the cybersecurity industry—consultants, engineers, incident responders, red teamers, researchers, regulators, and architects—this work is dedicated to you. Your generosity in sharing time, experience, and historical recollections has enriched every page of this book. Through revisiting old cases and challenging long-held assumptions, you have revealed that cybersecurity is as much a human endeavor as it is a technical one—a field where the line between defender and adversary blurs not by loyalty but by access, intent, and circumstance.

I offer my deepest gratitude to those who meticulously vetted stories, verified experiential accounts, and pushed for precision even when the myths sang a sweeter tune. Your insistence on accuracy and detail has not only refined the narrative but also strengthened the foundation upon which these chapters stand. For those who quickly responded to incidents, who wrote code on a moment's notice to make operations possible- I hope this book reflects the dynamic and complex world you have witnessed, shaped, and in thrive in.

This tribute is for the brilliant and creative minds who seek to understand how systems work—not solely to control and monitor them, or to gain greater insights into how they work, but also to reveal where the fissures and vulnerabilities lie. Your commitment to uncovering the intricate interplay between human intent and technological complexity is what drives our industry forward. Thank you for sharing your wisdom and your unwavering dedication to the art and science of cybersecurity.

Trusted by Design, Exposed by Convergence
Legacy OT in a Converged World: The Unraveling of Designed Trust

Table of Contents

Part IV – Strategic Tensions and Converged Defenses

Part V – Governance, Risk, and the Future of Industrial Protocols

About the Author

FOREWORD

There is a tendency—especially among those new to the discipline—to view cybersecurity as a domain of rapid iteration. Patching cycles, threat feeds, AI-enhanced detections, and zero-day disclosures all feed a constant churn. The tools evolve, the attackers adapt, and defenders pivot, again and again. But in the world of industrial systems, that rhythm breaks. Here, the clock moves slower. Not because the threats are absent—but because the systems were never built for this tempo in the first place.

That's what makes this book so essential.

Trusted by Design, Exposed by Convergence is not just a catalog of legacy protocol flaws or architectural oversights. It is an exploration of trust as it was originally imagined in industrial control systems—trust in physical separation, trust in limited access, trust in vendor designs, and trust in assumptions that were never meant to be questioned. This book does not cast blame. Instead, it performs the far more important work of illumination—exposing how that designed trust has fractured under the pressure of modern connectivity, remote access, supply chain interdependence, and adversarial persistence.

Bill Johns brings to this work not only a lifetime of field experience, but a historian's eye and a technician's clarity. The protocols are dissected, yes. But more importantly, the decisions that shaped them are understood—contextualized in the economic, operational, and cultural realities of the eras in which they were born. These are not just flaws in code; they are artifacts of a time when security was defined by location, not encryption.

You won't find hand-waving here. Each chapter draws a direct line from protocol to consequence. The stories are real. The vulnerabilities are lived. The environments—whether chemical, nuclear, or municipal—are fragile in ways that no glossy vendor whitepaper can gloss over. And yet, this book is not defeatist. It is strategic. Layered defense, protocol adaptation, digital twins, micro-segmentation, deception technologies, and cultural integration between OT and IT—all of these appear not as buzzwords, but as lived responses to systemic risk.

What makes this work most valuable, though, is its voice. There's empathy in these pages—for the engineer maintaining a 30-year-old PLC with no patch path; for the security analyst who sees the attack surface but lacks the authority to change it; for the vendors who inherited protocol stacks that were never meant to be public. This is a book written not to shame, but to equip. Not to dramatize, but to clarify.

It is, above all, honest.

For those securing the future of critical infrastructure—whether you are a policymaker, an operator, a red teamer, or an architect —this is the map you didn't know you needed. Not just a list of where the cracks are, but how they formed, why they matter, and what must be done before they give way completely.

The networks no longer operate in isolation. The enemies are no longer hypothetical. The convergence is not coming—it has already happened.

This book shows us how to respond.

PREFACE

This book is the product of long days in control rooms, of audits that turned up unexpected exposures, of offhand comments from veteran engineers that led down rabbit holes no one had charted. It was born from field notes and packet captures, from breached perimeters and legacy architectures that faltered under the pressure of modern interconnectivity. At its heart, *Trusted by Design, Exposed by Convergence* is not a condemnation of past design—it is an exploration of how assumptions once deemed safe have become silent vulnerabilities.

For decades, industrial control systems functioned on an implicit foundation of trust. Protocols spoke openly, devices obeyed without question, and security was measured in proximity rather than cryptography. This wasn't a mistake; it was a product of environment. In the context of isolated networks, vendor-specific hardware, and deterministic demands, trust wasn't just convenient—it was necessary. But the context changed. And trust, once a shortcut for performance, has become a liability.

What this book attempts to do is trace the ideological and technical lineage of insecurity—from protocols that were born before the internet, to the architectural decisions that wove them into modern networks, to the reasons why they remain prevalent today. It looks at convergence not as an abstract trend, but as a friction point: the moment when OT's emphasis on stability collided with IT's obsession with flexibility. And it asks what happens when that collision occurs on networks that control not just information, but infrastructure.

You can imagine the stories that are associated with each chapter. Sometimes it's a legacy device still humming along on borrowed time. Sometimes it's a red team exercise that veers into the realm of the absurd. Sometimes it's a protocol behaving exactly as it was designed—only now in a world that is no longer safe. The intent is not just to inform, but to frame these technical decisions in a human context. These were systems built by engineers, for engineers. They were tools of progress. Their flaws are not moral failings; they are the echoes of choices made with the best information available at the time.

But time has moved on. And so must we.

This book is written for those trying to secure what was never built to be defended—for the defenders inheriting networks without perimeters, for the architects trying to retrofit safety into fragility, and for the policymakers wrestling with regulation in a domain shaped by legacy. It is a book for anyone who has ever stared at an unauthenticated write command in a packet trace and realized just how little stood between an attacker and control.

In the pages ahead, you will find protocol analysis, historical reconstruction, technical commentary, and a heavy dose of realism. Some solutions will be offered. But many more questions will be raised—about governance, about interoperability, about how we decide which systems are too critical to fail, and yet leave them vulnerable by default.

If nothing else, I hope this work gives you a vocabulary for what you're seeing—and a framework for what might come next.

Because the network has enemies now. And the protocols still trust them.

INTRODUCTION –
TALKING IN THE CLEAR

It started with a packet capture—routine, unspectacular, part of a broader inspection of a control system's network health. A cybersecurity analyst at a North American energy provider, conducting a review of industrial network traffic, watched in real time as messages flowed between a control center HMI and a remote programmable logic controller (PLC). The protocol in use was Modbus/TCP—common, predictable, and, to many within operations, invisible. But as the analyst drilled into the payloads, what he saw wasn't subtle. There were no cryptographic handshakes. No credentials. No session tokens. Just raw, unauthenticated instructions, broadcast across the wire in plain ASCII. Write Coil. Read Register. Force Output. Commands flowing from trusted systems to obedient field devices, as if no one else could possibly be watching.

Except someone could. And in far too many industrial networks, someone often is.

This isn't about a rogue configuration or a misbehaving device. This is about behavior that is entirely by design. Industrial protocols—many of them developed in the 1970s, 80s, or 90s— were built on assumptions that, at the time, seemed reasonable: physical separation was security. Connectivity was controlled. Networks were private. The devices on them were purpose-built, expensive, and too obscure to be tampered with. The environment they operated in was never meant to be hostile – and at the time, there was little evidence to suggest that they were.

But time passed, and the environment changed. Ethernet

replaced serial lines. Internet Protocol routed what was once isolated. Windows replaced custom firmware as the common operating system of control centers. And industrial equipment, once shrouded in the air-gapped darkness of plant floors and substations, was pulled into the light of interconnected systems, supply chains, remote access platforms, and corporate networks. The protocols that these systems used—Modbus, DNP3, BACnet, PROFINET, EtherNet/IP, OPC Classic, and dozens of others—came along for the ride. But their architecture hadn't evolved. Their security models hadn't changed. The world around them had shifted into a battlefield. They were still trying to hold a polite conversation.

This book talks about some of those protocols, and what happens when they're asked to operate in a world they were never built to survive.

It's easy to attribute cybersecurity failures in industrial systems to malware, insider threats, or patching gaps. But the truth is deeper and far more uncomfortable. The weakest link is often not a human error or a software bug—it's the protocol itself. It's the default assumption that communication is allowed, that communication can be trusted. That devices will comply. That trust is implicit. That integrity doesn't need to be verified. In essence, many ICS and OT systems are talking in the clear— both literally, through unencrypted traffic, and philosophically, through architectures that assume good intentions.

Some of these flaws are well known, but often ignored. Others are poorly understood, even by defenders responsible for securing them. Most are invisible to traditional IT security tooling. And all of them exist at a layer of the stack that is difficult, if not impossible, to replace without re-engineering entire environments—power grids, water systems, factories, transport hubs. These are not web servers or email systems. These are critical infrastructures where uptime is sacred, and where risk is measured not in data loss, but in cascading physical consequences.

"Trusted by Design, Exposed by Convergence" explores this battlefield—not just as a technical landscape, but as a story of misaligned incentives, technological inertia, and the growing tension between availability and security. It begins with the origins of industrial communication protocols, when reliability and determinism reigned supreme and security was someone else's problem. It follows their awkward transition into the age of Ethernet and TCP/IP, where they were re-skinned and re-routed, but rarely re-designed. It examines real-world breaches have exploited these weaknesses—from Stuxnet's abuse of Siemens' internal protocols, to Industroyer's weaponized IEC-104 traffic, to red teams demonstrating privilege escalation over BACnet in modern building automation.

You'll encounter strange stories in the pages ahead: protocols that allow you to control physical equipment without so much as a login prompt; converters and gateways that serve as bridges between legacy and modern systems—and often between attacker and target; entire categories of critical devices whose firmware is incapable of enforcing even the most basic cryptographic protections.

But this book will also explore what can be done. It will look at how defenders are hardening legacy protocols with layered defenses: deep packet inspection, traffic shaping, software-defined segmentation, protocol-aware firewalls, and strict engineering controls. It will explore OPC UA's promise and its uneven adoption. It will discuss attempts to retrofit security into old protocols, and the economic and operational realities that often derail those efforts. And it will look to the future— what it might take to build protocols designed from the ground up for adversarial resilience.

Because in the end, the protocol is the language. And when the language itself is vulnerable, it doesn't matter how strong the walls are around it. Attackers don't need a zero-day if they have a key that's never been changed. They don't need to exploit firmware if the system is eager to comply with any well-formed command.

Security doesn't start with malware detection or endpoint control. In industrial systems, it starts with the conversations —the messages that pass unnoticed, uninspected, and often unprotected.

And right now, too many of those conversations are still happening in the clear.

PART I
Foundations of Fragility

CHAPTER 1 - A NETWORK WITHOUT ENEMIES

The control cabinet was older than the technician assigned to inspect it. Installed in 1998, it housed a PLC running a Modbus RTU stack over RS-485, still humming along faithfully as part of a high-throughput production line that had since been upgraded in nearly every other respect. Next to it, a touchscreen HMI streamed data to an edge server. Above it, sensors reported metrics over MQTT. But this controller—relic that it was—remained untouched. No encryption. No passwords. No integrity checks. It accepted commands from any Modbus master that could reach it on the wire. There was no malice in its design, no error in its implementation. They simply did what they had always done: listened and obeyed—with no judgment, no filtering, and no verification—just raw obedience.

And that is precisely the problem.

Across power plants, substations, wastewater facilities, food processing plants, mining operations, and steel mills, scenes like this play out every day. Equipment installed in the 1980s or 1990s still forms the backbone of operational technology environments. Remote terminal units, programmable logic controllers, distributed I/O modules, and intelligent electronic devices quietly execute their roles using communication stacks designed in an era before the internet reached the plant floor. These devices, still in service long past their intended life spans, now operate in a world of threats that didn't exist when they were conceived. Their protocols—frozen in time—reflect that original innocence.

The first PLCs appeared in the late 1960s, with Modicon's 084 often cited as the origin point of programmable industrial logic. Replacing hardwired relays with programmable ladder logic was revolutionary. Engineers could reconfigure a system's behavior by rewriting control sequences rather than rewiring physical circuits. The primary concern was deterministic operation—predictability, uptime, and resilience to failure. The idea of a malicious actor altering those control sequences remotely didn't even register. There were no outside actors. Security meant making sure the plant kept running and that hardware didn't fail under load. Communication between devices was achieved through proprietary, often undocumented, serial protocols hardwired over copper. Access to those lines was limited by the physical layout of the facility, which provided a passive but effective kind of defense.

In these environments, the concept of an air gap wasn't a security strategy—it was the natural architecture. Devices simply weren't connected to anything beyond the building. Engineering workstations sat on dedicated consoles with no uplinks. Human-machine interfaces ran vendor-specific operating systems, isolated by nature and not by design. Remote access was unheard of. Maintenance was performed on-site, with field engineers carrying diagnostic tools and configuration software to plug directly into a panel. Fieldbus networks such as Profibus, Foundation Fieldbus, and HART connected sensors and actuators, but these networks were never meant to leave the confines of the plant. They didn't need encryption or authentication because the only pathway into the system was a physical one.

And that assumption of isolation ran deep, shaping protocol design, physical architecture, and the very notion of what constituted a secure system. Protocols such as Modbus, released by Modicon in 1979, used a master-slave architecture that required no authentication. A Modbus master could read or write directly to registers on any slave device, with no handshake, no identity check, and no audit trail. This behavior was seen as a feature, not a flaw—simple, predictable, and easy to implement on limited hardware. The same principles were built into Profibus and later into DNP3, developed in the early 1990s for North American electric utilities. DNP3 offered advanced features like event buffering and time stamping, but it too operated on the presumption of trust. Even OPC Classic, which was developed to standardize communication between devices from different vendors, relied on Windows DCOM— a protocol that was never designed for secure use in open networks. These were protocols for a world without adversaries.

The illusion of security persisted not because of technological superiority, but because of physical separation. The air gap, never explicitly defined, acted as an invisible moat. This was not a world in which devices had firewalls, intrusion detection systems, or even the concept of a password on a controller. They didn't need them. The walls of the plant were considered sufficient. Security was locked doors, fenced perimeters, and the rarity of insider access. The systems themselves were not hardened because they weren't exposed. They were simply unreachable.

But reachability would soon change—not through attack, but through optimization. As organizations prioritized efficiency, visibility, and remote access, the walls around these systems quietly dissolved.

The world outside changed. With the rise of enterprise networking in the 1990s and early 2000s, operational networks began to adopt Ethernet and TCP/IP for the same reasons IT had: speed, interoperability, and cost savings. Vendors began shipping PLCs and RTUs with Ethernet ports. Protocols like Modbus were reimplemented for TCP. DNP3 was wrapped in IP for easier integration across wide-area utility networks. OPC was extended to allow remote access. SCADA systems grew more complex, increasingly deployed on general-purpose Windows machines. The convergence of IT and OT had begun, driven by a desire for centralization, visibility, and efficiency.

Initially, these changes seemed harmless. A PLC that could be remotely monitored reduced travel and allowed for faster diagnostics. SCADA servers that pushed data into corporate dashboards enabled predictive maintenance and higher-level oversight. Remote access tools reduced downtime during maintenance windows. But each of these improvements carried a hidden cost: they quietly eliminated the air gap. One Ethernet link at a time, one temporary VPN turned permanent, one field device with dual interfaces—these changes accumulated. The physical isolation on which these protocols had depended began to dissolve.

Yet the protocols didn't change. A Modbus device exposed over TCP still responded to any command sent its way. A DNP3 slave still accepted packets from any IP address that could reach it. BACnet systems in smart buildings still broadcast their presence on the network and trusted any device that could parse their messages. OPC Classic servers still opened up ports dynamically and relied on the security posture of the underlying Windows host, which often included remote desktop, SMB file shares, and active user sessions. The network perimeter had softened, but the protocols had not adapted. They still operated with the same open trust they had in the days of physical isolation.

The consequences of this exposure are not theoretical. As of early 2024, over 110,000 internet-facing industrial control devices were identified globally through active scanning. These included everything from building automation systems and manufacturing controllers to energy sector equipment. While the United States and Canada have made strides in reducing the number of exposed devices—down by more than 40 percent since 2017—other regions have trended sharply in the opposite direction. Countries like Spain, Italy, France, and Germany have all seen significant increases, with Spain's exposure rising by more than 80 percent over the same period.

The exposure of specific protocols tells an even more troubling story. Modbus, one of the most widely used protocols in industrial automation, has seen its presence on the public internet increase by nearly 50 percent since 2017. Siemens S7 devices, often used in high-value manufacturing and infrastructure, have more than doubled in exposure during the same period. These are not anomalies—they are indicators of a persistent structural issue, one where insecure protocols and long-lived devices are being pushed into network environments they were never meant to inhabit.

The longevity of industrial hardware plays a central role in this dilemma. A PLC installed in 1995 may still be under support, still functional, and still responsible for controlling a multi-million-dollar process line. Replacing that controller is rarely a simple swap. It may require reengineering the application code, validating timing responses, obtaining regulatory recertification, and re-training operators. In some regulated environments, such as pharmaceuticals or nuclear energy, this process could take months or even years. Worse, the replacement controller might still speak Modbus or DNP3, just with a newer firmware. The security model remains unchanged. Only the hardware gets a fresh label.

This situation has created a paradox. The most critical systems in society—those that power cities, treat drinking water, manufacture medicine, or refine fuel—are often the ones most dependent on protocols that have no ability to authenticate their traffic, validate message integrity, or resist replay. In penetration testing engagements, red teams have exploited these weaknesses to manipulate processes with no alerts or alarms. In some cases, they've been able to change setpoints, toggle valves, or simulate false readings with nothing more than a few packets and a knowledge of the protocol structure. No malware required. No exploit code. Just command syntax and network access.

Stuxnet demonstrated how deep knowledge of vendor-specific

protocols could be weaponized to sabotage physical systems. Industroyer showed that attackers could build custom modules to speak the native protocols of substation equipment. TRISIS exposed how safety instrumented systems could be subverted by understanding how firmware updates were delivered over engineering interfaces. These incidents were not purely about zero-day vulnerabilities in software—they were about the attackers' ability to speak the same language as the machinery and be understood. In each case, the protocol offered no resistance. The assumption of trust became the attacker's entry point.

The persistence of these insecure protocols is not a failure of individual engineers or plant operators. It is the result of an ecosystem built around long-lived devices, risk-averse operational models, and a near-complete inversion of IT security priorities. Where IT security values agility, OT security values stability. Where IT can afford disruption, OT often cannot. In OT, uptime is safety, and any change is a potential hazard. That culture, built over decades of keeping dangerous processes under control, now finds itself at odds with a threat landscape it was never designed to face.

The result is a foundation of communication protocols that continue to operate as if the network had no enemies, even as those enemies grow more capable, more persistent, and more aware of how to exploit that very trust.

This book will trace those protocols from origin to exploitation. It will examine how each was designed, how it operates, and how attackers have learned to manipulate it. It will explore how defenders are trying to retrofit security where none was originally intended and consider what a future protocol architecture might require if it hopes to survive in a hostile environment. But before we can secure the industrial world, we must first understand how it came to speak in languages that cannot say no.

BILL JOHNS

The network once had no enemies. But the enemies have come.
And the protocols are still wide open.

CHAPTER 2 - THE GREAT CONVERGENCE: IT MEETS OT

The blinking cursor on the Windows 95 SCADA terminal looked out of place, even back then. The engineer, used to working on DOS-based HMIs and serial-connected diagnostic tools, found it odd to be navigating process graphics with a mouse instead of function keys. But the vendor had promised a modernized experience—faster rendering, easier configuration, network visibility, and compatibility with standard IT infrastructure. The new system could export trends to Excel. It could be backed up over the LAN. It could even email alarms. It was the future of control systems. What no one said at the time was that this future came with risks no one in the control room had been trained to understand.

The rise of Ethernet and TCP/IP in industrial environments was not driven by security—or even by a clear understanding of risk—it was driven by convenience, cost, and the relentless gravitational pull of IT standardization. Until the late 1990s, most industrial control systems operated in tightly controlled serial environments. RS-232 and RS-485 lines carried traffic between human-machine interfaces and PLCs. Protocols like Modbus, Profibus, and DF1 chattered quietly in purpose-built physical loops. The network was not a factor. It was a wire, a voltage shift, a timing cycle. The idea of a routable infrastructure that linked control rooms to corporate offices, engineering workstations, and cloud dashboards was still largely conceptual.

But Ethernet was cheaper. And it was fast. And it was everywhere.

As enterprises embraced Ethernet and IP networking for business operations, pressure mounted to bring the same efficiency and visibility into plant environments. Industrial Ethernet—once an experimental curiosity—began appearing in vendor brochures. Controllers were shipped with RJ45 ports. The first wave of Windows-based HMIs and SCADA packages arrived with installers, not EEPROM cartridges. They ran on desktop-grade machines. They accepted mouse input. They integrated with Microsoft Office. The sales pitch wasn't subtle: reduce downtime, streamline operations, share data, standardize tools.

And it worked. At least, for a while.

Supervisory Control and Data Acquisition systems, once limited to centralized terminals, began to grow more complex and more connected. It became common to monitor remote substations or pump stations from a central location. Engineers started accessing systems offsite. Remote desktop access was set up for convenience. FTP servers were installed to move configuration files between departments. Firewalls were deployed—often with flat rulesets that permitted wide swaths of traffic across ports no one documented. The network, once an afterthought, had become the connective tissue of the entire operation.

But the protocols weren't ready.

Many of them, like DNP3, were originally designed to operate over serial links. DNP3, developed in the early 1990s for the electric utility industry, offered innovations like time synchronization, unsolicited messaging, and buffered events. It was optimized for noisy physical environments where signal loss and retransmission were normal. But it was also entirely unauthenticated. There was no native encryption. Messages could be spoofed or replayed without detection. When DNP3 was adapted for IP networks, its transport layer changed—but its assumptions did not. It still trusted the source. It still trusted the medium. And it still relied on the idea that whoever was speaking must be authorized to do so.

OPC Classic, originally intended to enable interoperability between Windows-based control applications and hardware drivers, introduced an entirely different kind of risk. Built on Microsoft's COM and DCOM architectures, OPC depended on dynamic port negotiation, process injection, and system-level permissions. These were not industrial design choices—they were artifacts of enterprise desktop environments. OPC allowed disparate systems to communicate using shared memory and method calls, which worked beautifully in local, isolated systems. But when extended over IP, it required open firewalls, registry configurations, and trust relationships between hosts —many of which were neither documented nor secured. In some cases, entire networks were reconfigured to accommodate OPC's needs, inadvertently weakening the isolation that once protected the control layer.

As these technologies proliferated, early signs of trouble began to surface. Broadcast storms, triggered by unmanaged switches or misconfigured protocols, overwhelmed fragile networks. Latency-sensitive control loops suffered as traffic increased, causing jitter, stalling PID controllers, or delaying critical interlocks. Engineers noticed system lag, not always realizing the root cause was excessive background chatter from file transfers, ping sweeps, or software updates. Devices that were never meant to handle asynchronous, non-deterministic Ethernet traffic began locking up under load.

More troubling were the firmware faults. Buffer overflows in embedded devices—once rare—became more common as input handling was exposed to new, malformed packet types. Devices that were perfectly reliable on serial lines began crashing when placed behind poorly configured network interfaces. Diagnostic services meant to simplify vendor support were left open and unauthenticated, reachable by anyone with access to the subnet.

And because many systems were vendor-integrated black boxes, operators often had no visibility into the vulnerabilities until something failed—sometimes during routine scans or maintenance windows, sometimes during a live process.

In one case, a utility substation went dark after a firmware update to a communication gateway exposed a flaw in its TCP stack. The update introduced a new diagnostic service that responded to malformed input by locking up the device entirely. It took hours to identify the cause, longer still to patch, and the only thing that prevented a cascading outage was a mechanical failsafe designed decades earlier. In another incident, a building management system froze under a broadcast storm caused by a rogue BACnet device flooding the network with repeated discovery requests. The result was a loss of ventilation, alarms that failed to trigger, and hours of downtime before the device was isolated.

These were not security incidents in the traditional sense. They weren't the result of nation-state attackers or advanced persistent threats. They were the natural consequences of architectural misalignment. The protocols had not been hardened. The devices had not been tested under adversarial conditions. The networks had not been designed for exposure. And yet, everything was moving toward greater interconnection.

What many early adopters didn't recognize at the time—and what remains a point of friction to this day—is that IT and OT are not just different disciplines. They are different worlds. The engineers who built the plant floor infrastructure came from a culture of safety, precision, and predictability. Their systems controlled physical outcomes—valves opening, breakers closing, motors spinning—and a mistake could trigger not just downtime, but real-world harm. They lived in a world where reliability was everything, change was inherently risky, and operational silence was a virtue.

IT practitioners, by contrast, came from a world of abstraction and speed. Their priorities were shaped by business continuity, data integrity, and user access. When IT adopted security as a formal discipline, it was around protecting data: email, intellectual property, customer records. Confidentiality and integrity were paramount. Downtime was inconvenient but recoverable. Updates were normal. Patching was expected.

So when IT security engineers began proposing defenses like endpoint detection, frequent patch cycles, or aggressive access control policies, they often ran headfirst into a wall of resistance from OT teams. What looked like good security hygiene to one group looked like operational sabotage to the other. OT engineers viewed security controls as potential sources of instability. IT saw resistance as negligence. Neither side was wrong. They were solving for different definitions of risk.

In a typical enterprise environment, the CIA triad—Confidentiality, Integrity, Availability—defines the pillars of security. But in OT, the order is reversed. Availability comes first. A system that is down—even for an update—is a failure. Integrity matters in the sense that a misconfigured PLC could cause a pump to stall or a turbine to surge. But confidentiality is often a distant third, especially in legacy environments where data theft is less dangerous than command misuse. That inversion of priorities reshapes every security conversation.

These cultural differences are compounded by the brutal mismatch in operational tempo. In enterprise IT environments, systems are built with the expectation of frequent change. Operating systems are patched weekly or monthly. Antivirus engines update daily. "Patch Tuesday" is a ritual. Downtime is planned and accepted, as long as it improves resilience or mitigates risk. If something breaks, it can often be restored from backup or rebuilt from a golden image. The assumption is that software evolves quickly and so must the defenses around it.

In OT, this cadence is not just impractical—it can

be catastrophic. Many industrial systems run continuously for years. Not metaphorically—literally years. Maintenance windows may be scheduled annually, or even less frequently, especially in regulated or high-throughput environments. A PLC controlling a bottling line may have logic untouched since 2004. A firmware update to a turbine controller may require months of planning, recertification, vendor oversight, and scheduled shutdown. And if the system is safety-rated, even minor configuration changes could trigger revalidation under regulatory regimes.

Because of this, many OT systems don't patch vulnerabilities at all. They isolate them, work around them, or document them. A known issue may remain in place for a decade—not because no one cares, but because touching it could cause more harm than leaving it alone. It's a world where risk is managed through predictability, not agility. And that worldview informs how OT engineers see protocols. If something works—no matter how insecure—it is preserved. If something changes, it is treated as a potential hazard.

That same principle extends to the tools used to identify and manage vulnerabilities. In enterprise IT, vulnerability management is typically built around detection and enforcement. Tools are designed to scan aggressively, patch automatically, and even quarantine assets that behave suspiciously. Anti-virus engines may terminate processes or block network ports when traffic patterns deviate from expected norms. Some endpoint protection platforms go further—disabling drivers, resetting services, or isolating hosts entirely based on heuristics or cloud-delivered threat intelligence.

In IT, that's expected behavior. In OT, it's a potential disaster.

One widely used antivirus platform, praised in corporate environments for its responsiveness, is known to shut down entire communication stacks when it encounters unexpected packet sequences. In a typical office network, that might interrupt a file transfer. On the plant floor, it might sever the link between a PLC and a motor controller mid-cycle. The software isn't malicious. It simply has no awareness of the deterministic protocols or timing constraints that define industrial systems. It sees Modbus and assumes it's a misbehaving device. It sees broadcast traffic and assumes it's a flood.

That's why OT vulnerability management is built differently. It has to be. Tools in industrial environments are designed to observe, not interfere. They catalog device types, firmware versions, communication patterns, and protocol usage— often passively, without injecting any traffic at all. When vulnerabilities are discovered, they are typically flagged, not fixed. Alerts are raised, but no automatic remediation is triggered. In many cases, a known vulnerability is documented and managed indefinitely because the cost of mitigation outweighs the risk of exploitation.

This is not a failure of strategy. It is a reflection of environment. In OT, security cannot come at the expense of safety. And any tool that does not understand the context of physical processes is more likely to cause harm than prevent it.

The great convergence of IT and OT brought visibility, efficiency, and capability—but it also brought exposure. It introduced a new kind of fragility, one rooted not in physical faults or operator error, but in protocol behavior that no longer matched its environment. These are not problems that can be patched at the edge or mitigated with firewalls alone. They are foundational. And they demand a reexamination not only of what we connect, but how we communicate when we do.

CHAPTER 3 - MODERN CYBERSECURITY FUNDAMENTALS

The modern digital landscape is a vast, interconnected ecosystem in which data flows seamlessly between devices, networks, and applications, demanding that every element —especially those governing critical industrial processes— be protected by robust, multifaceted security measures. As organizations have embraced digital transformation, the foundations of cybersecurity have shifted from static perimeters to dynamic, proactive defenses designed to respond to real-time threats. This evolution requires a fundamental rethinking of security principles, blending time-tested theories with emerging innovations to safeguard every potential point of vulnerability.

At the core of modern cybersecurity is the realization that no single defense is sufficient. Early security models relied heavily on physical isolation. In industrial settings, the air-gap was once considered an impenetrable boundary. Legacy OT systems, untouched by the internet and running deterministic routines, were believed to be safe by design. But the illusion of isolation was shattered by new threat vectors: compromised USB drives, vulnerable third-party vendors, and supply chain attacks that bypassed traditional barriers altogether.

This shift has led to a widespread adoption of defense-in-depth strategies. Rather than trusting a single line of defense, modern approaches wrap every system—especially legacy ones—in multiple layers of protection. Diodes, segmentation, advanced firewalls, intrusion detection systems, strict access controls, and continuous monitoring now form a concentric ring of defenses, each designed to compensate for the weaknesses of the others. Even if one layer fails, others remain active to protect the core. The concept of the air-gap didn't vanish—it evolved. Today, air-gapped systems are protected by layered architectures, both physical and logical, that grow more restrictive the closer they reach to critical assets.

Framing these defenses is the enduring CIA Triad—Confidentiality, Integrity, and Availability. In traditional IT systems, confidentiality and integrity dominate. Sensitive data must remain secret and unchanged, and breaches often mean reputational or financial harm. But in OT environments, availability takes precedence. A delayed or failed control signal can stop production or threaten safety. Data must still be accurate, but uptime is non-negotiable. OT environments require adaptations of the CIA model, where solutions prioritize availability while maintaining data integrity and applying confidentiality controls only when they don't interfere with operational continuity.

Legacy systems complicate these priorities. Designed for reliability, not security, they often run on minimal hardware, with little memory, custom operating systems, and no native encryption. Many operate on strict timing cycles that can be disrupted by even slight processing delays. A well-meaning security patch might introduce instability, desynchronize controls, or force revalidation of certified systems. These constraints demand careful, context-aware approaches.

Security teams have responded by offloading complex functions to external systems. Rather than forcing legacy devices to perform encryption or intrusion detection themselves, security gateways and monitoring appliances now serve as proxies. These external components handle encryption, validate traffic, and perform analytics while keeping the legacy system focused on its core function. This model creates a hybrid architecture—

reliable legacy at the core, protected by agile, modern security systems on the perimeter.

Technically, integration is difficult. Legacy systems must interface with complex modern infrastructure through custom middleware, protocol translation layers, and digital twins that allow for safe testing. These simulated environments replicate operational behavior to validate that new security controls don't interfere with timing, performance, or system stability. Without these precautions, well-intentioned security improvements can break the very systems they aim to protect.

Culturally, integration is harder still. OT engineers are trained for uptime, safety, and predictability. Their systems often reflect years of iterative tuning and deep process knowledge. The abrupt introduction of cybersecurity practices—with their jargon, update cycles, and apparent disregard for operational risk—can feel intrusive. Trust must be earned. Cross-functional teams that blend cybersecurity experts with OT veterans are vital. Shared vocabulary, mutual respect, and joint testing help bridge the cultural divide.

One of the most transformative shifts has been the adoption of continuous monitoring and real-time analytics. Cybersecurity was once reactive. Threats were dealt with after incidents occurred. Now, streaming data enables proactive detection. AI and machine learning systems parse network traffic and control signals, flagging anomalous behavior before it becomes dangerous. In ICS networks, where downtime can cost millions or endanger lives, this real-time insight is critical. Early alerts allow for surgical responses that isolate the problem without halting production.

This proactive model complements a zero-trust architecture— another foundational shift in cybersecurity thinking. Zero trust assumes no implicit trust, even for internal actors. Every access attempt is verified. Every signal is inspected. In legacy industrial systems, this represents a profound departure from past models where internal traffic was inherently trusted. Zero trust relies on granular authentication, micro-segmentation, least-privilege access, and real-time validation. It inserts friction into every interaction—but in doing so, it limits the adversary's ability to move laterally or escalate privilege inside a compromised network.

Together, defense-in-depth, continuous monitoring, and zero trust comprise the modern cybersecurity paradigm. It's a dynamic framework, constantly evaluated and refined as threats evolve. Regulatory standards have followed suit. Critical infrastructure operators are now expected to maintain detailed logs, conduct regular risk assessments, and validate security posture against industry benchmarks. Compliance is no longer a suggestion. It's a condition for operation. These standards have accelerated innovation, giving rise to security tools that balance control with compliance.

In this context, the CIA Triad becomes more than a theoretical model—it becomes an operational blueprint. Confidentiality must be respected, but not at the expense of availability. Integrity must be validated, not assumed. Every principle must be weighed against real-world constraints and tailored to the specific risks of industrial environments. Security cannot be allowed to impair function, nor can function be permitted to operate without security.

Achieving this balance requires more than technology. It demands alignment across engineering, operations, and cybersecurity teams. It calls for policy, training, documentation, and leadership support. The transformation of legacy systems into secure, modern components is not a one-time project. It is a sustained journey. It requires investment, iteration, and a willingness to challenge assumptions long held sacred in both IT and OT domains.

Modern cybersecurity is not just a defense mechanism—it is an enabler of resilience. It allows legacy systems to persist in a hostile environment. It acknowledges their limitations while providing tools to protect them. It fosters collaboration across disciplines and forces honest accounting of risk. And it creates a future where even the most trusted-by-design systems can be safely exposed in a converged, adversarial world.

The path forward is not easy. But it is clear. Cyber threats will grow. Legacy systems will endure. And the convergence of IT and OT will continue. Our responsibility is to ensure that this convergence does not become a collapse. Through layered defenses, adaptive monitoring, and an unrelenting commitment to zero trust, we can protect the critical infrastructure that powers our world—not by sealing it off, but by securing it within a new, resilient framework.

In this new era, legacy technology is no longer a liability to be hidden. It is a foundation to be secured. And cybersecurity is not a barrier to progress, but the means by which progress can safely continue.

CHAPTER 4 - HUMAN FACTORS AND INSIDER THREATS IN OT ENVIRONMENTS

There is a persistent myth that cybersecurity is purely a technical problem. Firewalls, encryption, air gaps, and patch management often dominate the conversation, especially in the world of industrial control systems. But anyone who has spent real time in operational environments knows that the human element is omnipresent. Behind every logic solver is a technician who programmed it. Behind every policy is a human judgment. And behind every breach—whether intentional or accidental— is someone who interacted with a system in a way that left it exposed. In legacy OT environments, where constraints are real and modernization is uneven, human behavior is not just a threat vector—it is often the primary one.

At a mid-sized energy facility, an operator once uploaded a previous version of logic to a safety controller, believing it to be the latest approved configuration. The system didn't fail immediately. It ran for weeks without issue. But under a rare yet predictable set of conditions, the outdated logic failed to trigger a safety shutdown. The fault was eventually caught, and disaster was narrowly avoided. It wasn't sabotage. No attacker was present. It was a simple case of poor version control, overconfidence, and absent procedural safeguards—yet it could have ended in catastrophe.

These kinds of incidents are not rare. They're endemic. They rarely make headlines and often aren't even classified as cyber events. But they form the blurry intersection where human performance meets system integrity. When a network is segmented, air-gapped, and monitored according to best practices—but still fails due to misjudgment or habit—it becomes clear that risk lives as much in culture as in code.

Insider threats in OT environments are not a single category. They span a spectrum: from the tired technician skipping a checklist step, to the disgruntled contractor with lingering root access, to the well-meaning engineer who clicks on a spear-phishing email disguised as a firmware update. These scenarios all bypass the traditional perimeter. They emerge from within the very trust fabric that industrial systems require to operate.

Legacy infrastructure intensifies the problem. Many systems were built before cybersecurity was even a consideration. Role-based access control may be nonexistent or disabled. Shared credentials are passed informally between shifts. Logging is limited or absent. Engineering workstations may double as general-purpose machines. It is not uncommon to find software from multiple vendors—decades of configuration remnants—coexisting with unpatched operating systems on machines essential to process safety. In such a setting, managing human risk becomes existential.

The most trusted personnel in a facility often hold the greatest potential for harm—not maliciously, but through habit, assumption, or improvisation. A technician who knows the system inside out might make undocumented changes to restore function quickly. The same familiarity that allows rapid response can also mask significant risk. Without checks, this access becomes a single point of failure.

Social engineering introduces another layer of complexity. Where physical access is restricted, attackers turn to psychological intrusion. Emails spoofing trusted vendors, loaded with malware disguised as configuration utilities, have entered OT environments more than once. So have phone calls posing as remote support, requesting temporary access for fake updates. On-site manipulation—tailgating, impersonation, badge-piggybacking—is also common in systems where trust is presumed and authentication is inconsistent.

Malicious insiders represent a quieter, but far more dangerous, category. They have the knowledge, credentials, and access to inflict lasting harm. In one documented but often misunderstood incident, a water treatment plant operator altered dosing pump configurations without authorization, risking chemical imbalances in public water. There was no malware involved—only inappropriate access. In facilities where audit logs are limited or nonexistent, intent is hard to determine and attribution becomes guesswork. By the time something seems wrong, damage may already be done.

The longstanding separation between IT and OT teams only widens the gap. IT departments may have well-defined access control processes, centralized logging, and security training programs. OT teams, particularly in legacy environments, often prioritize uptime over everything else. This divide creates blind spots. It also opens doors. A phishing email that would be quarantined on an enterprise server might sail through to a SCADA engineering terminal. A USB policy tightly enforced on corporate laptops may be completely absent from the field.

The underlying culture plays a decisive role. Engineers and technicians are natural problem solvers. If a tool slows them down or a workflow seems burdensome, they will find a workaround. These workarounds become habit. They become the unofficial standard. Over time, they embed themselves into the operational fabric, difficult to detect, harder to unwind. In this context, security is seen not as support, but as obstruction. The challenge lies in changing this perception without stripping away the autonomy and inventiveness that define these roles.

Reducing risk from human-originated threats requires

visibility, context, and cultural realignment. Behavioral analytics platforms, if used judiciously, can baseline activity and detect anomalies. If a contractor accesses systems at odd hours or a technician uploads configurations from an unfamiliar device, alarms can be raised. But these tools must be grounded in operational context. A behavior that seems suspicious during steady state may be normal during a turnaround. An alert that lacks nuance becomes noise. Analytics must be tuned—and they must be trusted.

Audit trails are foundational, yet many environments lack them. Legacy controllers may not support logging. Some devices overwrite their logs on reboot. When native visibility is impossible, alternate methods—network packet captures, historian correlation, workstation snapshots—must be used. Centralized logging, protected from tampering, is ideal. Without it, investigations become speculative. Even benign mistakes leave no trace. Malicious acts go unseen.

Structure helps. Tasks involving sensitive systems should be governed by formal procedures. Well-designed checklists reduce reliance on memory and help prevent errors caused by fatigue or distraction. For high-impact changes, a second layer of review can be applied. One person performs the task, another independently verifies the result. This double checklist method enforces accuracy and reinforces accountability.

In high-consequence environments, the two-person rule is standard. Requiring two qualified individuals to be present and involved—whether uploading logic, initiating firmware updates, or modifying interlocks—provides both oversight and redundancy. Separation of duties is a powerful deterrent. When no single actor can execute changes alone, the opportunity for sabotage or error is minimized. Dual-approval workflows, change management gates, and peer reviews slow the process down—but in the right way. This is friction designed for safety. If the process is too rigid, it will be bypassed. The goal is to integrate validation into workflows without breaking them.

Training is essential, but it must be meaningful. Security briefings pulled from IT slideshows won't resonate with field personnel. OT training must be grounded in the realities of operations. What does a malicious firmware email look like? Why is plugging in an unvetted USB dangerous? The scenarios must be real, relatable, and updated frequently. Short, situational refreshers tied to plant events or seasonal work cycles are more effective than once-a-year seminars.

Where contract labor or vendor access is frequent, onboarding and offboarding become security linchpins. Contractor accounts should not linger. Access rights must be clearly defined and tightly controlled. When a project ends, access must end with it. Without formal deprovisioning, access becomes a drifting concept. Likewise, old logic files or configuration backups in the hands of former staff may remain accurate—and exploitable— long after their departure. Identity lifecycle management isn't just a convenience—it's a necessity.

Most of all, organizations must foster a culture where accountability does not equate to punishment. When mistakes are met with blame, they go unreported. Lessons are lost. The same error repeats. A blameless postmortem approach— focused on understanding, prevention, and shared learning— encourages openness. It turns near misses into case studies. It builds a security mindset not from fear, but from ownership.

In the best environments, security becomes a shared language. Cross-functional teams of IT cybersecurity professionals and OT engineers learn to navigate one another's worlds. At first, the partnership may be strained. IT professionals bring speed, automation, and policy. OT engineers bring experience, physical risk awareness, and deep system intuition. These are not just different disciplines—they are different cognitive frames. And yet, over time, collaboration leads to translation. IT learns protocol nuance and uptime dependencies. OT learns the risk calculus and value of visibility. They stop debating whether a system should be patched. They design mitigations that account for uptime and security. Controls are not imposed—they're co-developed. The result is more resilient and more aligned with reality.

The human firewall is not a metaphor. It's a reality. Every operator, engineer, and contractor is either a point of risk or a line of defense. Which role they play depends on the systems, policies, and culture around them. Technology alone will not secure legacy OT environments. Trust must be earned, workflows must be validated, and human behavior must be supported—not constrained. The future of OT cybersecurity depends not only on code, but on people. The human factor is not the problem. It is the solution—if we treat it that way.

CHAPTER 5 - BRIDGING THE DIVIDE: ALIGNING OT REALITIES WITH IT SECURITY IMPERATIVES

When industrial control systems were first conceived in the mid-20th century, engineers designed networks for power plants, chemical facilities, and manufacturing lines with the simple notion that physical isolation meant security. In those early systems, the control room was a sanctum—a place where carefully designed, air-gapped networks operated under the assumption that devices confined to a closed environment were inherently trusted and would never be attacked. Security was not an active discipline but rather an implicit consequence of isolation. Protocols such as the analog 4–20 mA current loop, early fieldbuses like Profibus, and proprietary control languages were engineered for reliability, determinism, and long operational lifespans. Their very design assumed that if you had physical access to the equipment, trust was automatic. This model worked well in an era when connectivity was minimal and the idea of a remote adversary was far-fetched. In that environment, even if data were transmitted without encryption or authentication, the sheer isolation of these networks provided sufficient protection.

In stark contrast, the world of Information Technology (IT) evolved in an era where every data packet is treated with suspicion. IT security professionals work with technologies that incorporate encryption, authenticated sessions, and rapid patch cycles, continuously reinforcing a dynamic, risk-aware environment. The modern IT realm is built upon a foundation of protocols standardized to defend against a myriad of digital adversaries and complex threat models.

Yet this expertise in IT rarely extends to the realm of operational technology (OT), where engineers manage systems that "just work" through legacy protocols that were never designed with contemporary cyber threats in mind. This divergence in expertise and philosophy has created a profound disconnect between the two domains—a gap that modern industrial enterprises must bridge in order to secure their critical infrastructures.

OT engineers have spent decades maintaining systems whose primary objectives are reliability and continuity. Whether it is the robust simplicity of the 4–20 mA current loop, the predictable operation of Profibus networks, or the straightforward communication of the Siemens S7 protocol, these systems were designed in a world where physical access implied trust and sophisticated cyber threats were not a consideration. Because OT protocols were built for environments focused on uninterrupted operation, they lack the cryptographic handshakes and dynamic challenge–response mechanisms that are standard in IT. In OT, the emphasis has always been on ensuring that control commands are executed accurately and on schedule, even if that means sacrificing an inherent layer of digital security.

This fundamental difference is further underscored by the contrasting patch and refresh cycles in the two domains. In the IT world, patch cycles are rapid and dynamic—security teams roll out updates on a weekly or monthly basis to counter emerging threats. Hardware refreshes occur every few years, driven by a relentless pursuit of enhanced performance and the latest security features. IT systems are, by their nature, agile and designed for rapid adaptation in the face of evolving cyber risks.

In contrast, OT environments operate on markedly different

timelines. Maintenance and patch cycles in OT are far more deliberate and infrequent, often stretching into years. The criticality of the processes they control, coupled with stringent safety and certification requirements, means that any change can carry significant operational—and even safety—risks. Industrial equipment is engineered to last for decades, and the inherent reluctance to disrupt processes that have reliably functioned for extended periods makes proactive vulnerability management and strategic modernization particularly challenging. In this environment, the hardware, firmware, software and protocols may be decades old, not standardized, and no longer available or supported. Patching and refreshes may not even be possible at all. And certainly not without considerable risk to production and safety – and not without considerable planning, testing and expense.

The disparity between external and internal threat and risk models further deepens the divide. IT cybersecurity professionals are accustomed to concentrating on adversaries at the perimeter—sophisticated hackers, nation-state actors, and cybercriminal groups that exploit vulnerabilities visible on the internet or through corporate networks. Their risk models emphasize the relentless external probing of networks, deploying firewalls, intrusion detection systems, and rapid patch cycles as primary defenses. They invest heavily in firewalls, intrusion detection systems, and rapid patch cycles because their operating assumptions are that attackers are constantly probing for a weak link from afar. In this world, the risk is defined by what an external actor can accomplish, whether that's through phishing, remote exploitation, or malware infiltration. Additionally, resilience strategies include regular backups of each critical device – making recovery relatively uncomplicated to accomplish.

In stark contrast, OT engineers are primarily concerned with threats that originate from within their industrial environment. For OT professionals, the most critical risks involve internal misconfigurations, human error, and unintended operational changes that can disrupt critical production processes. Their systems—often decades old, designed with minimal connectivity, and optimized for reliability—are vulnerable to disturbances that originate from within: a misapplied patch, unauthorized device access by a disgruntled insider, or even inadvertent changes in the configuration that ripple through a network and cause process anomalies. In an environment where even a minor disruption can lead to production loss, safety hazards, or significant downtime, OT security focuses on internal controls, rigorous change management, and continuous monitoring of device behavior in real time. Most devices, and OT protocols don't include backup capabilities, and recovery from an incident would be extremely time consuming and expensive, particularly if the attack results in physical damage. For example, the Stuxnet attack on Natanz occurred in 2009 and 2010. While it is difficult to pinpoint when Natanz recovered from this attack, it wasn't until 2021 that IAEA suggested that Natanz seemed to almost fully recover.

This fundamental difference in risk focus means that IT and OT teams sometimes have conflicting perspectives on what constitutes a threat and the appropriate response. While IT may invest resources in countering attacks that breach the outer network layers, OT must pay closer attention to internal controls, monitoring critical device behavior in real time, and ensuring that the environment remains stable even as changes occur. In the OT world, security is not just about keeping outsiders out; it is equally about maintaining the integrity and continuity of production processes from within an environment where even small disruptions can have significant consequences.

Bridging the divide between IT and OT requires more than just technical integration—it demands a shift in mindset and the creation of a common language of risk that acknowledges the unique challenges of each domain. As industrial networks become increasingly interconnected, the old model of relying solely on a physical air-gap is no longer viable. Critical OT systems, which were once safely isolated, now sit alongside IT infrastructure in complex, multi-layered architectures. The challenge is to secure these systems by developing an integrated strategy that embraces both the legacy wisdom of OT and the agile, proactive approaches of IT.

At the heart of this integrated strategy lies the recognition that modern cyber defense for industrial systems must be built around a defense-in-depth approach. Legacy protocols, by their very nature, cannot be retrofitted with security features like modern cryptographic protections or authentication methods without a complete overhaul—which is neither practical nor economically feasible for many installations. Instead, these systems must be enveloped within concentric layers of security controls.

This begins with ensuring that the critical systems that govern industrial processes are physically hardened and isolated as much as possible within the modern network. At the core of this strategy are the systems that directly govern industrial processes—hardened workstations, dedicated networks, and meticulously controlled communication channels. Surrounding these critical systems are additional layers such as diodes, firewalls, intrusion detection systems, and continuous monitoring tools. Each layer is designed not to be perfect in isolation, but to work in concert so that if one layer is breached, the next continues to provide protection, thereby safeguarding the overall confidentiality, integrity, and availability of operations. Yet, physical isolation alone is not enough. Logical segmentation of networks is critical: by dividing the infrastructure into secure zones, organizations can restrict the lateral movement of an adversary, preventing a breach in one area from cascading into the entire system.

Continuous monitoring is an indispensable element of this layered defense. Since many legacy protocols lack built-in security features, the reliance on meticulous, real-time monitoring becomes vital. Modern monitoring tools offer continuous asset management, advanced anomaly detection, and behavioral baselining to detect deviations from established operational norms. The introduction of digital twins and simulation technologies further enhances this capability by enabling operators to model control processes and detect when sensor outputs diverge from expected patterns. This not only transforms static networks into agile, adaptive defenses but also provides the early warning necessary to trigger a rapid incident response before minor anomalies become major disruptions.

Another essential dimension of bridging the divide is fostering collaboration between OT and IT teams. It is not uncommon for IT professionals, with their focus on rapid patch cycles and dynamic threat responses, to propose measures that may, in the OT context, be disruptive. Conversely, OT engineers may view IT-driven security changes as intrusive alterations that compromise system stability. Successful industrial organizations have recognized that the key to a unified cyber defense is the creation of joint incident response teams, cross-disciplinary training programs, and integrated asset management platforms. These initiatives help forge a shared understanding and language of security, ensuring that the imperatives of rapid digital defense can coexist with the need for long-term operational stability. When IT professionals understand that industrial systems cannot tolerate rapid, untested changes, and when OT engineers become familiar with the techniques of continuous monitoring and rapid incident response, a unified risk posture emerges—one that respects both the legacy reliability of OT and the adaptive defenses of modern IT.

The cultural divide between IT and OT often stems from their differing interpretations of risk. For IT, the primary focus is on defending against external threats through encryption, multifactor authentication, and an almost continuous cycle of updates and patches. For OT, the emphasis is on ensuring that control commands are executed accurately and in a timely manner, where even minor disruptions can have tangible, dangerous consequences. This difference requires a nuanced approach to security—a strategy that recognizes that not every connection needs the same level of digital hardening, but that every layer must be continuously validated. By tailoring defense measures to the unique needs of industrial environments— where the stakes are physical and production continuity is critical—organizations can implement a strategy that builds resilience without compromising operational effectiveness.

Another component of this integrated approach is understanding the economic and practical realities of the industrial world. Many industrial facilities have relied on legacy systems for decades because they are proven to work, and the cost and risk associated with overhauling these systems are enormous. Downtime, recertification, and retraining represent significant expenses that often deter operators from embracing rapid changes. Yet, the long-term cost of inaction in today's threat environment may far exceed the investments required for modernization. As such, the convergence of OT and IT must also account for the economic models that justify gradual, non-disruptive modernization. Instead of a wholesale replacement, the strategy must be one of incremental, carefully managed updates—each step verified through rigorous testing and closely monitored for any signs of instability or security weakness.

A critical part of this integrated strategy is recognizing that OT engineers may not be fully versed in the sophisticated details of modern IT protocols. Although many IT practitioners are experts in dynamic, encrypted communications, they frequently lack hands-on experience with the decades-old protocols used on the plant floor. This gap in practical knowledge can result in IT security measures that are theoretically sound but operationally disruptive. Conversely, OT engineers, whose systems have been built on the assumption of a benign, isolated environment, sometimes view IT-driven security changes as unwelcome disruptions that jeopardize system stability. Thus, bridging the divide requires both sides to appreciate each other's constraints—for IT, understanding that industrial systems demand a slow, methodical approach to change, and for OT, recognizing that modern threats call for continuous, proactive security measures.

At the heart of these efforts is a need to reinterpret the CIA triad for industrial environments. In IT, confidentiality and integrity dominate the design of protocols, ensuring that data is kept secret and unaltered during transmission. In OT, integrity and availability are paramount—what matters most is that control commands are executed accurately and in a timely manner, even if the data itself is not encrypted. Modern industrial security must reconcile these differences by building layered defenses that protect critical assets even when some traditional elements of security are absent. This means establishing multiple concentric rings of defense around the most critical systems, where every connection from the sensor to the supervisory control remains validated and continuously monitored.

Successful organizations are already beginning to build this bridge through collaborative initiatives such as joint incident response teams, cross-disciplinary training programs, and integrated asset management platforms. In one instance, an industrial facility implemented a continuous, real-time inventory system by combining tools like Tenable OT, Claroty, and Nozomi Networks. This system not only mapped every connected sensor and gateway, but also correlated any changes against historical baselines and emerging threat intelligence. When an anomaly—a misconfigured 4–20 gateway blending signals from a decommissioned sensor with those of an active one—was detected, the integrated team worked together to swiftly remediate the issue before it could escalate into a safety hazard. In another case, an automotive plant conducted joint red-team exercises, where IT and OT professionals simulated attacks against legacy protocols and collaboratively reviewed the outcomes. These exercises revealed that conventional IT security measures, if applied too rigidly, could inadvertently disrupt critical control processes. Through these initiatives, the two cultures began to converge on a common, unified risk posture.

The path forward, therefore, is one of continuous evolution —a strategy built on the integration of longstanding OT reliability with the advanced threat detection and rapid response mechanisms of IT. At every layer of defense, from physical security measures guarding wiring and terminal blocks to logical segmentation techniques that create robust network islands, there must be continuous validation. Every transaction, every data flow from sensor to digital gateway, must be monitored, correlated, and evaluated against a baseline of known safe behavior. This multi-layered monitoring is not merely a passive process; it is the active engine of security in an environment where legacy systems cannot be retrofitted with modern protections.

To illustrate the success of this integrated strategy, consider an industrial facility that implemented a continuous, real-time inventory system using technologies from leading vendors such as Tenable OT, Claroty, and Nozomi Networks. This system not only mapped every connected sensor and gateway but also correlated any changes against historical baselines and current threat intelligence. When an anomaly was detected— such as a misconfigured 4–20 mA gateway that blended signals from both decommissioned and active sensors—the integrated team was able to rapidly respond, isolating the potential fault before it escalated into a safety hazard. In another instance, an automotive plant conducted joint red-team exercises in which IT and OT professionals simulated attacks against legacy protocols. These exercises revealed that overly rigid application of IT security measures could inadvertently disrupt critical control processes. However, through collaborative review and adaptation, the teams developed a unified, nuanced security posture that balanced digital defense with operational continuity.

Every layer of this defense requires constant attention. The physical security of a facility remains as crucial as ever— protecting connection points and wiring from tampering is the first step in a multi-layered strategy. Logical segmentation must be aggressively enforced, ensuring that if one layer is compromised, the breach does not propagate to critical areas. Continuous monitoring, enabled by advanced digital twins and real-time analytics, ensures that any deviation from expected behavior triggers immediate investigation. In this integrated model, automated alerts are paired with human oversight, and every response is calibrated to minimize operational disruption while maximizing security.

Ultimately, bridging the divide between OT and IT is about converging two very different worldviews—one that values uninterrupted, predictable operation and another that prioritizes dynamic, continually updated security measures. It is a process of mutual education and collaboration, of building joint incident response teams and sharing cross-disciplinary expertise. Through continuous, real-time monitoring and a defense-in-depth strategy that layers physical, logical, and operational controls, organizations can protect their critical industrial processes without sacrificing reliability.

The future of industrial cybersecurity depends on this integration—on embedding legacy systems within a comprehensive, multi-layered defense architecture that recognizes the intrinsic limitations of old protocols while capitalizing on modern threat intelligence and rapid response capabilities. By aligning the operational realities of OT with the advanced methodologies of IT, organizations can build resilient infrastructures that safeguard both the physical processes driving industry and the digital networks that govern them.

This strategy does not prescribe a one-size-fits-all solution. Rather, it calls for a tailored approach, one that acknowledges the unique challenges and constraints of each operational environment. It is an ongoing process of adaptation and improvement—a commitment to continuous monitoring, joint training, and shared responsibility that will ultimately secure the critical infrastructure of our industrial future. In this integrated approach, every link in the network, from the analog sensor wire to the digital gateway and beyond, is continuously validated and protected against emerging threats. Only by embracing this holistic, layered defense—in which the traditional trust of OT is reinforced by the vigilant, adaptive capabilities of IT—can organizations hope to safeguard their legacy systems against the relentless forces of modern cyber threats.

CHAPTER 6 - TRUST ON THE WIRE: LEGACY ASSUMPTIONS IN A NETWORKED AGE

The first time a control room operator was told that their PLCs were accessible via a browser, the reaction was disbelief. Not anger. Not fear. Just confusion. The system in question had been running flawlessly for years, monitored from a secure terminal inside a fenced facility. But during a routine network review, an external cybersecurity consultant discovered that one of the vendor-supplied PLCs was accessible from the corporate network—complete with an embedded web server for diagnostics and configuration. The controller had no login screen, no SSL certificate, and no logging. The interface was there, waiting, because no one had thought to turn it off. And in many cases, no one knew it was there in the first place.

The controller wasn't misconfigured. It was functioning exactly as it was designed to. It was built to be helpful.

This is the story of how operational systems, once defined by isolation and trust, became networked without ever learning how to say no. It is the story of protocols that made the leap from serial to Ethernet, from proprietary to IP-based, but brought their trust models with them like baggage from another era. And it is the story of a slow-motion collision between two worlds—information technology and operational technology—each with its own assumptions about speed, risk, and resilience.

For much of their history, industrial protocols were quiet. They moved over twisted-pair cabling in polling cycles measured in milliseconds. They were rarely logged, almost never inspected, and not expected to handle exceptions beyond broken wires or checksum errors. The systems they powered were simple, reliable, and highly specialized. Engineers designed them with physical layouts in mind. A message from the master to a slave was expected to cross a single wire, reach a known address, and return with a value from a register or a status bit. The idea that such traffic would someday traverse an IP-routable network was unimaginable.

But in the late 1990s and early 2000s, industrial systems underwent a quiet revolution. The price of Ethernet hardware plummeted. TCP/IP had become the lingua franca of enterprise communication. Microsoft Windows was now the standard operating environment for SCADA systems and HMIs. And vendors—eager to meet demands for centralized monitoring, predictive analytics, and remote maintenance—began layering IP transport into their products. What followed was not so much a redesign as a repackaging. Protocols like Modbus, DNP3, and OPC were wrapped for TCP/IP transport, assigned default ports, and made accessible over switched networks. These were engineering solutions, not security decisions.

The problem was that in many cases, the protocols were lifted out of their old context but never recontextualized. Modbus/TCP, for instance, remained functionally identical to its serial predecessor. The master could still read or write to any register without authentication. The difference was that the messages now traveled through infrastructure designed for email and web traffic, across routers and switches that made the PLC indistinguishable from a printer or file server. And because it worked—and because uptime was paramount—there was no compelling reason to change it.

At first, these changes seemed beneficial. A technician no longer needed to walk the plant floor to check device status. Remote facilities could be monitored from a centralized location.

Engineers could download logic changes over VPN, cutting down on travel time and response lag. Data historians began collecting massive volumes of telemetry, pushing it upstream to corporate IT for analysis. Production became smarter, leaner, more responsive. The business value was real, and the technology delivered it.

What no one noticed at the time was that the new convenience came with a cost. When a protocol designed for physical adjacency is placed on a network where every device is potentially remote, the assumption of trust becomes an open door. And in the case of industrial protocols, there was no doorframe, no peephole, not even a lock. There was simply a message, transmitted in clear text, accepted without question.

The conversion from serial to Ethernet was never about security —it was about speed and scale. Gateways were introduced to bridge serial segments to IP, but most simply encapsulated frames without inspecting them. PLCs began to ship with dual Ethernet ports, but few included packet filtering or access control logic. Devices advertised their services via broadcast protocols, eager to be found, and often configured with vendor default credentials—if any credentials at all. Engineers, trained to think in terms of electrical faults and process variables, had no reason to suspect that the protocol stack itself could be a vector for compromise.

Even as vendors added new features—web servers, FTP access, SNMP, REST APIs—these were seen as value-adds, not risk factors. Configuration interfaces were often bolted directly onto the control path. In some cases, the same port used for firmware updates could also issue start or stop commands to the process. Engineers loved the flexibility. Plant managers appreciated the visibility. Security, if considered at all, was assumed to reside at the perimeter. These features were often added with no consideration for cryptographic protections. When vendors enabled FTP for firmware updates or configuration file transfers, it wasn't secure FTP. It was the original, unauthenticated, plaintext FTP protocol—transmitting login credentials and sensitive files in the clear. Similarly, embedded web servers rarely used HTTPS. They served diagnostics or control interfaces over plain HTTP, sometimes hardcoded to default ports, sometimes unable to support encryption at all. The inclusion of these services wasn't a mistake. It was seen as progress—tools to make management easier. But they were implemented in a way that assumed privacy through obscurity, not through cryptographic assurance. In doing so, they created silent attack surfaces, invisible until someone went looking.

In many cases, the engineers building these products weren't trying to cut corners. They were solving real operational problems. Vendors added features because customers asked for them. Management prioritized functionality and time-to-market. Secure design wasn't ignored—it simply wasn't part of the design vocabulary. Security was still seen as a property of the network, not the protocol or device itself. If an embedded system could be patched or upgraded to add HTTPS support, it often meant rewriting firmware or changing hardware, which few vendors were willing to do unless a customer was loudly demanding it. In most cases, the demand never came.

The first cracks in this model appeared quietly. A misconfigured firewall. A forgotten NAT rule. A shared switch between two different trust zones. One energy company discovered that a diagnostic service enabled for vendor maintenance had been quietly relaying Modbus traffic from a test bench into the main production network. Another uncovered an HMI system running on an aging Windows XP box that shared a network segment with a file server used by HR. No one had connected the dots. These systems hadn't been targeted, but they were exposed. And if someone had known where to look, they would have found industrial systems talking in the clear, accepting unauthenticated commands on well-known ports.

As plant and enterprise networks continued to converge, segmentation blurred. In some facilities, HMI terminals shared switches with accounting workstations. In others, an unsecured file share was used to pass configuration files between departments. Vendor support often required remote desktop sessions, sometimes left active for weeks. Portable engineering laptops moved freely between zones. And everywhere, the protocols kept talking—unauthenticated, unencrypted, and unconcerned with who might be listening.

The danger wasn't that these systems were failing. The danger was that they were functioning exactly as designed.

It's easy to miss how pervasive the assumptions of trust really are in legacy protocols. Consider BACnet, used in building automation. By design, it allows devices to broadcast their capabilities, respond to queries, and accept commands from any system that knows how to speak the language. That makes integration simple. It also makes impersonation trivial. While efforts such as BACnet Secure Connect (BACnet/SC) have been introduced to address these concerns through encryption and mutual authentication, adoption remains inconsistent and many deployments still rely on the unauthenticated default behavior. Or take DNP3, which supports unsolicited messaging and bulk data transfer—features that increase performance, but also enable crafted payloads to overwhelm or mislead. And then there's OPC Classic, which uses dynamic ports, Windows authentication inheritance, and COM/DCOM object referencing —creating a labyrinth of dependencies ripe for exploitation. These behaviors aren't bugs. They're features optimized for a world without adversaries.

The security community has long emphasized the principle of least privilege, but industrial protocols are often built around the opposite assumption: that all connected nodes are trusted, well-behaved peers. This stems not from ignorance, but from the original operating context. In a serial network, connected devices were hardwired. They didn't move. They weren't added without intent. The idea that a rogue node might appear mid-cycle with malicious commands wasn't a use case engineers considered. So, the protocols didn't include the logic to handle that case. And once they were moved onto IP networks, those same protocols had no way of enforcing privilege boundaries or verifying message authenticity.

Some defenders attempted to adapt by segmenting networks —placing critical devices on VLANs, enforcing access controls through firewalls, building out industrial demilitarized zones. In theory, these mitigations should have worked. But in practice, they were fragile. A misconfigured rule set. A switch port in the wrong VLAN. A technician bridging zones with a dual-homed laptop. In environments where uptime is prioritized above all else, complex segmentation schemes tend to erode. Over time, many networks that looked secure on paper became flat again in reality. And the protocols within them remained unchanged, silently granting access to anyone who could speak their language.

The legacy lives on. Today, many ICS networks still operate as if the messages themselves are inherently valid—as if anything that arrives on the right port, in the right format, must be legitimate. This is why protocol-aware firewalls, anomaly detection engines, and deep packet inspection tools are now essential in environments where the underlying protocols cannot be trusted to defend themselves. But these tools are compensatory. They exist because the protocols are blind to intent.

This blind spot has consequences. It invites attackers to blend in. An adversary who understands how to craft a Modbus write command doesn't need to exploit a buffer overflow—they just need a foothold on the network. A misconfigured gateway, an exposed diagnostic port, or an overlooked test device becomes a vector. And because the message looks normal, most defenses won't flag it. The protocol was never taught the difference between a good command and a malicious one. It just sees bytes. And it obeys.

The convergence of IT and OT has delivered incredible operational benefits. But it has also exposed a fundamental mismatch between the assumptions of legacy protocols and the realities of modern threat environments. We are no longer in a world where the network has no enemies. Yet much of our infrastructure still communicates as if it does.

This chapter began with a simple example—a PLC with a web interface exposed to an internal network. It ends with a deeper truth. The problem isn't that the device was vulnerable. It's that the protocol made no distinction between friend and foe, user and attacker, engineer and intruder. It trusted the wire.

The chapters ahead will dive into the specifics of these protocols —how they work, how they fail, how their trust assumptions shape everything around them, and how attackers exploit their trust. The core lesson has already emerged. When you bring a protocol built for cooperation into a world shaped by adversaries, what you get is not interoperability. When a protocol assumes the network is safe, every byte becomes a potential compromise. And as the convergence continues, that assumption becomes less tenable with every passing day.

PART II
Protocols That Never Learned to Defend Themselves

CHAPTER 7 - MODBUS: THE PROTOCOL THAT WOULDN'T DIE

The message is short. Eight bytes. A unit identifier, a function code, a register address, and a value. No handshake. No certificate. No authentication or authorization. Just a raw instruction from a master device to a slave, asking for a coil to be set, a register to be read, or a value to be overwritten. It's the same message structure that's been in use since 1979, and in many environments, it still controls pumps, motors, valves, and circuit breakers. The elegance of Modbus lies in its simplicity, and so does its danger.

Originally developed by Modicon—now part of Schneider Electric—Modbus was created to facilitate communication between industrial devices like PLCs, sensors, and operator terminals. It was never meant to be a security protocol. It wasn't even meant to be a network protocol in the modern sense. It was built for RS-232 and RS-485 serial communication, environments where cabling distances were short, devices were hardwired, and access was controlled by physical proximity. In that world, the protocol's simplicity was an asset. You didn't need a stack of libraries or a multi-threaded runtime to talk Modbus. You just needed a hex editor and a data sheet.

That simplicity is why Modbus caught on so quickly. It was open, easily implemented, and agnostic to the specific vendor hardware underneath. As manufacturers looked to integrate different types of field devices into SCADA environments, Modbus became the common denominator—a lingua franca of automation. Entire generations of engineers learned to read Modbus function codes by heart. And because it was so widely supported, it became the default choice for many integrations, even when better or more secure alternatives were available.

In its original form, Modbus used a master-slave model. A master device issued commands, and slave devices responded. Only the master initiated communication. The slaves waited silently, performing whatever instruction they were given. There was no built-in mechanism for verifying whether a command was legitimate, nor any way for a slave to reject a well-formed message based on source. In the serial context, that wasn't seen as a flaw. If you had access to the RS-485 bus, you were assumed to be trusted. There was no concept of an adversarial network. The wire was the boundary.

That boundary dissolved with the arrival of Ethernet. As industrial networks adopted TCP/IP, Modbus was adapted accordingly. The result was Modbus/TCP, which encapsulated the original Modbus frame inside a TCP packet and transmitted it across routable networks. Functionally, the behavior was nearly identical—the master sent a command, and the slave responded. But the context had changed dramatically. Now the master could be located anywhere on the same network segment. Or on a different subnet. Or on the other side of a NAT. Or, with a misconfigured firewall, anywhere on the public internet.

Yet the protocol itself didn't evolve. Modbus/TCP made no changes to the security model. It added no authentication, no session management, no encryption, no integrity checking. The slave still accepted commands from any IP address that could reach port 502. If the message was well-formed, it was accepted and executed. There was no awareness of source identity, no validation of operator intent, and no audit trail of activity. The protocol still assumed a trustworthy wire, even as that wire had become a web of interconnected systems with unknown endpoints.

As with many legacy protocols, this was not a deliberate act of negligence—it was inertia. Modbus worked. It was embedded in firmware. It was included in product documentation. Customers expected it. And vendors were reluctant to break compatibility. Even when more secure alternatives were available—such as OPC UA or vendor-specific encrypted APIs—Modbus remained the default fallback, especially for configuration, diagnostics, and local integration tasks. In many environments, new devices are still shipped with Modbus/TCP enabled by default, often with no password, no logging, and no access controls beyond the network perimeter.

Despite its age, Modbus is not just a legacy holdover—it is still being actively deployed. Vendors include it because customers ask for it. Integrators favor it because it just works. And in environments where simplicity and cost control are paramount, Modbus often wins by default. Even in greenfield projects, it shows up—sometimes as a primary interface, sometimes as a hidden diagnostic backdoor. Its reputation for reliability keeps it alive, even when security concerns would suggest it should be retired.

The consequences of this are both predictable and disturbing. In vulnerability assessments and red-team engagements, Modbus is often one of the first protocols checked for exposure. It's easily discovered—many devices broadcast their availability using standard TCP port 502, and scanners like Nmap or Shodan can identify Modbus endpoints with minimal effort. Once found, the devices respond with register maps, coil states, and in some cases, full memory contents. There are no login prompts. There is no obfuscation. The data is available to anyone who knows how to ask.

Shodan regularly indexes tens of thousands of internet-accessible Modbus devices. Some are honeypots, but many are real—water pumps, refrigeration units, generators, irrigation controls, and even municipal power infrastructure. As of early 2024, more than 110,000 internet-facing industrial control systems had been cataloged across various platforms, with Modbus accounting for nearly a third of all exposed services. Independent research from operational technology firms placed the global total of Modbus-exposed ICS devices at over 46,000, not including devices behind weakly secured gateways or remote desktop sessions that allow indirect access. The threat is not speculative—it is ongoing, mapped, and expanding.

Modbus is a favorite target in industrial honeypot research. In some environments, Modbus is not actively used by automation logic, but left enabled as a configuration channel. A technician might connect once a year to change a register. But between those moments, the service remains open, listening silently on the network. In studies conducted by government and industry observers, Modbus consistently ranks among the most scanned and manipulated protocols on honeypot infrastructure. Attackers probe register ranges, flip coils, and flood devices with malformed messages. Sometimes it's automated scanning. Other times, it's clearly manual and methodical—testing for human response.

Even when not used for direct control, Modbus serves as a convenient reconnaissance channel. With function codes like 0x03 (read holding registers) or 0x2B (read device identification), adversaries can learn which devices are online, what firmware they run, and whether they're part of redundant failover pairs. This activity doesn't trip alarms because it resembles normal SCADA polling. But in the hands of an attacker, it lays the groundwork for precision targeting.

More critically, Modbus allows direct control of physical processes. An attacker doesn't need to exploit a vulnerability or bypass a firewall. They only need to issue a legitimate Modbus write command. With access to the network and knowledge of the register map—which can often be deduced or found online— they can start or stop pumps, change flow setpoints, alter relay positions, or inject bad values into sensors. Because the protocol provides no way to distinguish legitimate commands from malicious ones, the system simply does what it is told. It obeys.

There have been documented cases where Modbus was used to disrupt or manipulate industrial environments, not as the result of malware, but as the result of unauthorized access. In one incident, a disgruntled contractor with VPN credentials was able to change control logic remotely by injecting Modbus commands into the SCADA network. In another, a misconfigured gateway bridged the corporate and control networks, exposing a battery management system to public internet traffic. Within days, the Modbus controller was receiving invalid commands from unknown sources—some exploratory, others clearly malicious.

In hybrid environments, Modbus often exists alongside more modern protocols like OPC UA or BACnet. The result is a split-stack security model: telemetry is protected, but control is not. A system might encrypt every sensor reading and timestamp, while allowing any internal node to issue raw Modbus writes. The illusion of safety breaks down the moment an attacker speaks the right language on the wrong side of the network.

Part of Modbus's fragility comes from the devices themselves. Most Modbus-speaking PLCs do not support access control lists. Any request that reaches port 502 is accepted without question. There are no user roles, no time-of-day constraints, no per-command throttling. The device will respond to as many commands as it receives, as fast as they arrive. If the traffic is malformed or abusive, the result may be instability, crashing, or silent misbehavior.

Modbus/RTU, the original serial variant, remains common in systems where physical separation is still in place. But in most environments, those serial links are now terminated at gateways that convert the protocol to Modbus/TCP. These gateways act as bridges between legacy serial infrastructure and modern IP networks. But they rarely inspect the content of the messages. Most perform a simple pass-through, relaying requests from the IP side to the serial bus without modification or scrutiny. If a malicious actor can reach the gateway, they can reach the downstream devices.

These gateways also introduce new risks. Many are themselves embedded systems with minimal security hardening. Some have default credentials, open web interfaces, or outdated firmware. Others are configured with overly permissive rules, allowing any source to communicate with any downstream slave. In more than a few cases, field assessments have revealed dual-homed gateways with one interface on the control network and the other on a wireless access point or public-facing management VLAN. The very tools used to modernize infrastructure often become the points of failure.

Broadcast behavior introduces yet another variable. While Modbus/RTU allows for broadcast messages to address all slaves simultaneously, Modbus/TCP support for broadcasts is inconsistent. Some devices ignore them. Others process them without logging. This creates ambiguity during integration and danger during incident response. In one real-world scenario, a broadcast message intended to update only a redundancy heartbeat was interpreted by nearby devices as a system-wide failover trigger—causing a switchover that wasn't needed and wasn't reversed until manually reset.

Even obscure function codes carry risk. Code 0x08, intended for loopback diagnostics, is rarely used in production, but allows for internal counters to be cleared or devices to be reset. It's a perfect tool for an attacker who doesn't want to break a system—just to confuse it or knock it offline for a few minutes. Other rarely used codes behave differently across devices, opening a wide and unpredictable surface for abuse.

Modbus is entirely stateless. There's no concept of session negotiation, no replay detection, no nonce or sequence validation. A packet captured once can be replayed indefinitely with identical effect. Protocol-aware defenses must monitor traffic not just for content, but for timing and repetition, a challenge made more difficult by how deterministic legitimate Modbus traffic often is. This lack of context-awareness makes it nearly impossible to determine whether a command was triggered by a human operator or injected by an adversary already inside the network.

Defenders have tried to compensate. Network segmentation is often cited as the first line of defense—isolating Modbus devices onto their own VLANs or control zones and limiting access via ACLs or firewalls. This works in theory, but in practice, segmentation is frequently incomplete or misconfigured. In large environments, it's not uncommon to find engineering workstations or vendor support laptops with access to both the control and enterprise networks. Portable devices used for diagnostics may carry infections or bridge trust boundaries inadvertently. And because Modbus is so tolerant of poor design, these configurations rarely break functionality.

Some modern control systems attempt to wrap Modbus traffic inside encrypted tunnels—typically via VPNs or SSH—but this is a stopgap. It protects the traffic in transit but does nothing to secure the protocol itself. The message remains unauthenticated at the application layer. If a VPN credential is compromised, or if the endpoint is already on the inside, the protection vanishes. Other defenders rely on protocol-aware firewalls or intrusion detection systems that can parse Modbus traffic and alert on suspicious commands. These tools can be effective, especially when combined with deep packet inspection and behavioral baselining. But they are reactive. They detect abuse; they do not prevent it.

Efforts have been made to develop secure variants of Modbus, but adoption has been limited. Modbus Security, a specification published by the Modbus Organization, defines extensions for authentication, encryption, and message integrity using TLS. But the adoption curve is shallow. Devices in the field do not support it, and retrofitting them is often not possible. The interoperability that made Modbus so attractive in the first place now becomes a liability. Secure extensions break compatibility. Vendors hesitate. Users default to what works.

During the 2016 cyberattack on Ukraine's power grid, the malware framework known as Industroyer—or CrashOverride —used Modbus directly to manipulate substation control equipment. It didn't exploit the protocol. It spoke it fluently. Like an insider with root access, it simply issued commands that the devices could not question. That attack was a warning: that protocols obey, even when they shouldn't. And Modbus is no exception.

The reality is that Modbus continues to exist not because it is secure, but because it is simple, predictable, and universally understood. That simplicity has allowed it to survive for over four decades, spanning from the era of serial punch-through cables to modern cloud-connected control environments. It is the protocol that won't die because it was never designed to live in the world it now occupies. And yet, it does.

As defenders, we are left with the uncomfortable truth that Modbus must often be protected from the outside in. It cannot defend itself. It cannot challenge a command, verify a source, or audit a session. It listens. It responds. It trusts. Every time it is allowed onto a routable network without compensating controls, it represents an open gate in the perimeter—one that cannot be closed from within.

Understanding how Modbus operates, where it fails, and how it continues to be abused is not just academic. It is a prerequisite for securing the real world—because Modbus doesn't just control devices. It controls consequences.

And it is still everywhere.

CHAPTER 8 - OPC AND THE DANGER OF INTEROPERABILITY

It started with a good idea. A simple one, really. Operators and engineers were tired of proprietary drivers, brittle integrations, and hand-coded interfaces just to connect a human-machine interface to a programmable logic controller. Every vendor had their own protocol, their own library, their own quirks. If you wanted to switch brands or add a new device to your control architecture, you had to recompile your software or install yet another vendor runtime. Interoperability was an illusion. The process was fragile, time-consuming, and expensive.

In 1996, the OPC Foundation proposed something radical: a standardized interface based on Microsoft technologies that would allow disparate industrial systems to communicate using a common API. The goal was abstraction. If every device could expose its data through the same software layer, then software vendors could build visualization, logging, and automation systems that would work across manufacturers. The result was OPC Classic—short for OLE for Process Control—a clever repurposing of Microsoft's Object Linking and Embedding technology to wrap industrial data in a familiar, Windows-native container.

It worked. And it changed everything.

Suddenly, developers could write a generic OPC client and connect it to any vendor's OPC server. Instead of parsing raw serial packets or managing proprietary memory maps, applications could browse available tags, subscribe to updates, and write values through a clean, COM-based interface. OPC became the de facto standard for Windows-based interoperability in industrial environments. Vendors embraced it, integrators relied on it, and thousands of control systems were built with OPC Classic at their core. It was, for a time, the most successful standardization effort in the history of industrial automation.

But there was a catch. OPC Classic was not an industrial protocol. It was a software interface built on technologies designed for enterprise desktops—not safety-critical environments. It inherited the architecture of Microsoft's Component Object Model and Distributed Component Object Model—COM and DCOM—which were designed in an era where software components were expected to run on the same machine or, at most, in a local domain with shared trust and administrative access. The underlying assumption was that all parties were cooperative, trusted, and part of the same security boundary.

In the context of industrial systems, this assumption proved disastrous.

DCOM allowed OPC clients and servers to communicate across machines, enabling remote access and distributed architectures. But it did so by relying on a deeply complex stack of inter-process communication mechanisms, dynamic port negotiation, and privilege inheritance. When an OPC client requested a connection to a remote server, DCOM would negotiate a random port above 1024 for communication, then attempt to instantiate objects on the target machine using the security context of the calling process—or, if improperly configured, the system account. This behavior was convenient for enterprise applications that trusted each other. In OT environments, it became a liability.

Firewalls struggled to accommodate OPC. Because DCOM used dynamic ports, administrators either had to open a wide swath of ephemeral ports—exposing the machine to numerous other threats—or hardcode a port range and hope the applications complied. In practice, this meant that many control systems ran with permissive firewall rules or, more often, with firewalls disabled entirely between trusted nodes. Worse, because OPC traffic piggybacked on Windows RPC mechanisms, intrusion detection systems had little ability to distinguish between valid industrial commands and rogue administrative operations. The protocol surface was sprawling, opaque, and ripe for abuse.

Privilege inheritance created even greater risk. A client process running as an administrator could instantiate remote objects with elevated privileges. In some configurations, simply requesting a connection to an OPC server could trigger the execution of code in the system context. The very features that made OPC powerful—automatic marshaling, deep integration with the OS, rich callback mechanisms—also made it brittle and dangerous. If a client was compromised, the server could be next. And because many OPC servers ran on engineering workstations, historian servers, or SCADA hosts, the blast radius was significant.

Beyond basic misuse, DCOM provides attackers with powerful tools for exploitation. Through specially crafted RPC requests, adversaries can trigger remote DLL loading, execute arbitrary COM objects in the context of system services, and perform memory injection across trust boundaries. These techniques are well documented in penetration testing frameworks and have been used in targeted campaigns. In a flat or poorly segmented OT domain, the presence of an OPC server may be the attacker's stepping stone to the crown jewels—not because OPC is broken, but because the trust model around it was never designed to resist intrusion.

These problems were not theoretical. During red team assessments and forensic investigations, OPC Classic has frequently been a point of lateral movement. Once inside a network, attackers look for machines running OPC servers, knowing they are likely to accept remote connections without much scrutiny. By exploiting DCOM behavior or misconfigurations in access permissions, they can pivot from one trusted node to another—often invisibly. In some cases, malware has used OPC as a transport layer, embedding payloads inside OPC calls to evade detection.

The operational implications are just as severe. Many control environments rely on OPC for real-time data sharing between systems. If a historian can no longer connect to a PLC, or if a visualization client loses its OPC session, operators lose visibility. This makes OPC a high-value target—not just for attackers, but for system integrators trying to optimize plant behavior. The irony is that the same architecture that made integration easy also made disruption easy.

Engineers often find themselves boxed in. They can't remove OPC because critical processes depend on it. They can't secure it without breaking compatibility. And they can't replace it overnight because the migration path is long, costly, and fraught with uncertainty. The result is a generation of industrial systems that rely on software interfaces designed for a different time, operating in environments that were never part of the original threat model.

Over time, workarounds emerged. Vendors published whitepapers on how to lock down DCOM, restrict port ranges, and harden OPC server configurations. Microsoft introduced group policy templates and registry tweaks to control DCOM behavior more granularly. But these changes required deep knowledge of Windows internals, and few operators were willing to risk making those changes in production. In many cases, the guidance went unread. The default configurations remained. And so did the vulnerabilities.

Some defenders attempted segmentation—placing OPC servers in isolated VLANs and using terminal services to access them indirectly. Others deployed protocol-aware firewalls or application-layer proxies to sanitize traffic. A few organizations invested in security gateways that could monitor OPC behavior and terminate sessions that appeared anomalous. But this introduces a risk of its own. In production environments, particularly those tied to safety systems or high-reliability processes, terminating an active session can be more dangerous than allowing a suspicious one to proceed. A firewall that drops a malformed packet mid-transaction may leave a process hanging, a screen frozen, or a controller stuck in a half-updated state. In industrial settings, silence is not neutral—it is a fault condition. A well-intentioned defense mechanism that cuts off communication can become the very source of the failure it's trying to prevent.

This is the uncomfortable trade-off that emerges when security and reliability collide. Visibility is essential. Logging is non-negotiable. But enforcement must be handled with the kind of caution usually reserved for emergency stops and fail-safe relays. The protocol may be insecure, but the infrastructure around it must be fault-tolerant—and that means watching more often than intervening. In OT, the tools that merely observe are often safer than the ones that act.

To avoid the complexity of DCOM without giving up OPC Classic, many asset owners turned to tunneling products. These tools encapsulate OPC traffic inside proprietary TCP or HTTP tunnels, allowing clients and servers to communicate across firewalls without modifying COM settings or opening dynamic ports. While they solve the DCOM problem on paper, they introduce new problems of their own. Many tunnels bypass Windows authentication entirely, rely on shared secrets, or enforce no real access control at all. They simplify integration but obscure visibility. And they create a second-order trust model that rarely matches the security assumptions of the host network.

These tunneling solutions also complicate incident response. When a system relies on proprietary encapsulation, defenders must understand not only the OPC traffic but also the vendor-specific wrapper. In the event of an intrusion, forensic teams may find themselves staring at TCP payloads that carry opaque, binary-encoded messages for which no documentation exists. What was meant to streamline security ends up complicating it, sometimes to the point of paralysis.

In environments where data must flow in only one direction —such as nuclear facilities or defense sectors—OPC Classic has never fit cleanly. Its stateful, bidirectional model does not align with data diode architectures. Organizations have been forced to engineer intermediate layers: staging servers that poll devices, buffer the data, and re-transmit it in unidirectional form. These intermediary systems increase complexity and introduce their own failure modes. OPC UA, with its support for stateless reads and service-oriented models, is a better fit, but many of these high-security environments are slow to adopt new technology. As a result, OPC Classic continues to persist in places where its architectural model is most misaligned with the risk tolerance of the environment.

In 2022, Microsoft began disabling DCOM by default across supported versions of Windows. This change—intended to address longstanding security issues—caught many industrial operators off guard. OPC Classic implementations that had functioned reliably for decades began failing silently after routine patches. In some cases, integrators were forced to roll back system updates. In others, entire migration projects were launched in response to unexpected outages. The situation exposed a painful truth: many organizations had no idea just how deeply embedded DCOM was in their operations until it was taken away. The very patch intended to improve security became the catalyst for disruption.

The DCOM hardening saga illustrates the irreconcilable tension between IT's need to patch and OT's need for stability. To enterprise administrators, disabling a legacy service is responsible hygiene. To OT engineers, it's an unplanned intervention in a tightly coupled system. In response, some vendors issued hotfixes to re-enable DCOM temporarily. Others advised leaving systems unpatched. Neither option was ideal. But both were chosen, depending on which risk the organization was more willing to accept—security debt or functional uncertainty.

As the limitations of OPC Classic became impossible to ignore, the OPC Foundation began work on a successor. The result was OPC Unified Architecture—OPC UA—a complete redesign of the protocol with modern security principles in mind. Unlike its predecessor, OPC UA was platform-independent, supporting both Windows and non-Windows environments. It eliminated the reliance on COM and DCOM, instead using a binary TCP-based protocol or HTTP with SOAP/XML, depending on the use case. Most importantly, OPC UA included support for authentication, encryption, and integrity checking out of the box.

In theory, OPC UA solved the problems that plagued OPC Classic. In practice, adoption has been slow. Part of the issue is compatibility. OPC UA is not a drop-in replacement. Clients and servers must be rewritten or wrapped in compatibility layers. Legacy devices that only support OPC Classic cannot be retrofitted. Vendors that built their product lines around COM-based interfaces must redesign their software stacks. And integrators with limited budgets are reluctant to rip and replace systems that are still operational.

Even in environments that have adopted OPC UA, security features are not always enabled. It is possible—common, even —for OPC UA servers to be deployed without certificates, or with encryption disabled for performance reasons. Many organizations prioritize interoperability over security, enabling features that allow Classic clients to connect to UA servers, effectively recreating the same weaknesses that UA was meant to eliminate. The flexibility of OPC UA is both a strength and a risk—it can be deployed securely, but it doesn't enforce security.

As a result, many industrial environments are caught in an uneasy middle ground. They still rely on OPC Classic for core functionality, even as they experiment with OPC UA in pilot projects. They expose DCOM to enable legacy integrations, while attempting to segment or monitor the resulting traffic. They know the risks, but they also know the costs. And in critical systems, change is never trivial.

The persistence of OPC Classic is a reminder that interoperability is a double-edged sword. What makes systems work together can also make them fail together. A single interface shared across vendors creates a single point of failure, a single surface of attack, and a single mechanism by which a compromise can propagate. And when that interface is deeply tied to the operating system, the consequences extend beyond process control—they reach into system stability, administrative boundaries, and domain trust models.

There is no question that OPC Classic was a revolutionary technology. It enabled a generation of automation that would have been impossible without it. But it also imported the weaknesses of the IT world into environments that were not prepared to handle them. It assumed trust where none existed. It assumed compatibility where none could be guaranteed. And it assumed that Windows-based security models could stretch to cover real-time, high-stakes control systems without tearing at the seams.

The path forward is not simple. OPC UA represents progress, but not a cure-all. Secure deployment still requires configuration, training, and discipline. Legacy systems will not disappear overnight. And for many organizations, the burden of change will remain higher than the perceived risk—until an incident proves otherwise. What OPC teaches us, more than anything, is that convenience and security are often at odds. And in the world of industrial automation, the price of convenience can be measured in risk that accumulates quietly until it becomes unavoidable.

The danger of interoperability is not in the idea itself, but in the details of its implementation. When we make systems talk to each other, we must also ask how they listen, how they authenticate, how they decide who to trust, and how they fail when those assumptions are violated. OPC Classic made it easy to connect the world. And in doing so, it made it just as easy to compromise it. That is the lesson we carry forward—not to fear interoperability, but to respect its power. Because when it is built on a shaky foundation, even the best intentions can become the biggest vulnerabilities.

And no one will care how elegant the architecture was when the process stops, the screen goes black, and the system that trusted too much suddenly has nothing left to say.

CHAPTER 9 - DNP3: DESIGNED FOR TRUST, DEPLOYED FOR RISK

In the mid-1990s, as the electric utility industry sought to modernize and unify its control systems, a new protocol quietly emerged from a landscape cluttered with vendor-specific implementations and serial line hacks. That protocol was DNP3 —the Distributed Network Protocol version 3—and it was designed not just to address the chaos of the past but to provide structure, consistency, and performance across a fragmented industry. It wasn't a reinvention of the wheel. It was a careful evolution of it—one that prioritized determinism, efficiency, and trust in equal measure.

DNP3 was not built for the internet. It wasn't even built with the internet in mind. It came from an era where remote terminal units sat at substations, data concentrators polled them over leased lines, and timing was measured in tens of milliseconds. The first deployments ran over serial links—RS-232, RS-485, even copper twisted pairs laid across hardened infrastructure. Security came not from cryptography but from geography. If you could reach the cable, you were trusted. If you couldn't, you weren't a threat. This assumption, unspoken but foundational, would shape the protocol's behavior in ways that would become liabilities decades later.

The design of DNP3 was elegant in its own right. Unlike earlier protocols that focused solely on command-response exchanges, DNP3 introduced features that were ahead of their time. It supported event buffering, which allowed outstations to retain data changes until the master polled for them. It could prioritize critical data, reducing unnecessary traffic in bandwidth-constrained environments. It allowed unsolicited responses, giving outstations the ability to push updates to the master without being polled—useful for alarms, fault conditions, or rapidly changing states. And it was layered, following the OSI model more faithfully than many of its contemporaries, which made implementation cleaner and behavior more predictable.

Compared to protocols like Modbus, DNP3 was a leap forward. It supported multi-layer encapsulation, confirmed messaging, time synchronization, and prioritized buffering. It wasn't dumb, and it wasn't rushed. That's what makes its modern misuse so frustrating. It was never meant to be abused, only trusted. But trust doesn't scale across networks—and it certainly doesn't survive exposure to the internet.

But at its core, DNP3 was built on trust. Messages were assumed to come from authorized sources. There was no authentication of the sender, no encryption of the payload, and no signature to confirm integrity. Sequence numbers helped with replay protection to a limited degree, but there was no cryptographic barrier against tampering. DNP3 expected that if you were on the wire, you belonged there. And for a while, that assumption was enough.

Then came the network.

As utilities began to replace point-to-point serial links with TCP/IP transport, DNP3 was adapted to follow. The serial frame was encapsulated in TCP, port 20000 was standardized for transport, and suddenly DNP3 could be routed over internal networks—or across leased lines, MPLS backbones, and, in some cases, even the open internet. What hadn't changed was the protocol itself. The same messages were still accepted, still acted upon, and still unauthenticated. The wire had gotten longer, but the rules hadn't. The trust remained.

This adaptation brought tremendous operational convenience.

Utilities could manage hundreds of substations from a central control center. Field devices could be reconfigured, reset, or diagnosed remotely. Event logs could be pulled on demand, and firmware updates delivered over the air. But every advantage came with an equal and opposite exposure. Because DNP3 had no built-in security model, it relied entirely on the assumption that the network itself was trustworthy—or at least adequately segmented from anything dangerous. This was rarely true in practice.

Flat internal networks, misconfigured firewalls, and VPN concentrators with wide access became the unwitting gateways into control infrastructure. The moment an attacker or piece of malware gained a foothold on the inside, DNP3 was exposed —not by flaw, but by design. The protocol's minimalism became a vulnerability. There were no passwords to crack, no certificates to spoof. If a host could reach port 20000, and if it spoke the protocol correctly, the messages would be accepted and processed. This was not a bug. This was the operational expectation.

The exposure wasn't just theoretical. In multiple penetration tests and real-world breaches, attackers used unauthenticated DNP3 messages to request data dumps, flip bits, reset counters, and flood logging systems. In one documented case, a security audit of a municipal utility revealed that dozens of field devices were reachable over a cellular modem interface, with DNP3 exposed directly to the public internet. The devices responded politely to every query, offering up coil status, configuration values, and even internal clock times to any unauthenticated connection. There was no malware, no exploit code—just a complete absence of boundary.

As of early 2024, global scans by Censys identified over 145,000 internet-facing ICS services, with more than 48,000 in the United States alone. While not all of these represent DNP3 endpoints, the protocol remains disproportionately represented in North American utility networks. This means a nontrivial portion of those exposed systems are likely speaking DNP3 across unsecured networks—often unaware of the extent to which they are reachable, let alone vulnerable.

The message structure itself was simple and extensible. Each DNP3 message consisted of a header followed by objects—data structures representing inputs, outputs, counters, analog values, or control commands. The protocol used function codes to define behavior: read, write, select-before-operate, delay measurements, cold restart. These codes were powerful, particularly the control functions. Select-before-operate, for instance, required a master to send a "select" followed by an "operate" within a short window—a mechanism meant to reduce accidental actuation. But there was no protection against malicious or spoofed select/operate pairs.

Unsolicited messaging, one of DNP3's more advanced features, was designed to allow outstations to report changes without being polled. In high-speed utility environments, this was a breakthrough—it meant alarms could propagate faster and bandwidth could be conserved. But it also meant that endpoints could push data upstream at will. In a compromised network, unsolicited messaging can be weaponized to flood masters with noise, create false alarms, or overwhelm buffer capacities. Without filtering or throttling, a single rogue device can generate a flood of spurious events, degrading system performance or masking genuine issues behind a wall of noise.

One subtle risk with DNP3 lies in its support for fragmented messaging—an accommodation for low-bandwidth or constrained networks. Messages can be split across multiple frames, requiring the receiver to reassemble them before interpretation. In legacy or embedded implementations, improper fragment reassembly has led to crashes, memory exhaustion, and even remote code execution. Protocol-aware firewalls often struggle with deep inspection of fragmented DNP3 streams, particularly when the fragments are malformed or intentionally obfuscated. In adversarial hands, what was meant to improve reliability becomes an attack vector.

The rise of asset discovery engines like Shodan and Censys brought another layer of exposure. Internet-facing DNP3 services began showing up in public search indices. Some were honeypots, but many were real. In 2018, a survey found more than 600 DNP3 endpoints globally with no authentication or access controls. By 2022, the number had increased, not because more utilities were being careless, but because more devices were being connected—and few were designed to withstand scrutiny. Some vendors began hardening their firmware, but legacy deployments lagged far behind. Patching wasn't always an option. In many cases, operators didn't even know what firmware version they were running.

Efforts to secure DNP3 were already underway by the early 2000s. The result was Secure DNP3, a cryptographically enhanced version of the protocol that introduced authentication, integrity checking, and optional encryption. Secure DNP3 used a challenge-response mechanism to verify message origin, added HMACs for integrity, and supported session keys to prevent replay attacks. It didn't fix everything, but it addressed the most glaring weaknesses—particularly the assumption that any node with access to the network was inherently trustworthy.

Even when Secure DNP3 is adopted, verifying its proper implementation remains difficult. Many monitoring tools do not parse the cryptographic layers or validate session behavior. Security teams may assume protection is in place when in fact, shared keys or fallback behaviors are quietly disabling it. Until tooling catches up—and vendors enforce stricter defaults —Secure DNP3 will remain secure only in theory, not in deployment.

Adoption of Secure DNP3 has often been driven more by regulatory mandate than operational foresight. In North America, NERC CIP standards apply to certain classes of electric utilities but often exclude distribution-level assets or smaller co-ops, leaving wide gaps in enforcement. Internationally, IEC 62351 offers guidance for securing communication protocols like DNP3, but implementation remains voluntary in most regions. Until security becomes a procurement requirement—or a compliance checkpoint—many asset owners will continue to prioritize uptime and interoperability over cryptographic assurance.

The adoption of Secure DNP3, where it exists, has been slow and uneven. Part of the problem is interoperability. Legacy devices don't support it. Gateways often strip security features during conversion. And many utilities operate under regulatory regimes that prioritize availability and reliability over proactive cybersecurity investment. Enabling Secure DNP3 can require firmware updates, retraining staff, or replacing hardware outright. And where multiple vendors are involved, differences in implementation can lead to unpredictable behavior. As a result, many deployments continue to use legacy DNP3, relying on VPNs or firewalls to protect the perimeter—a brittle and insufficient model in the face of advanced threats or internal compromise.

In case studies from critical infrastructure incidents, DNP3 has often been present—not always as the vector of compromise, but as a silent enabler of deeper access. During one red team engagement against a regional transmission operator, testers gained access to the SCADA network via a misconfigured wireless bridge. Once inside, they found a DNP3 gateway connected to the transmission control center. The gateway had no ACLs and responded to queries from any internal host. By crafting read requests, the team extracted real-time breaker status, analog telemetry, and setpoint values. Write operations were blocked by configuration, but read access alone was enough to build a detailed map of grid topology, with time-aligned data suitable for operational modeling or even sabotage planning. The protocol had done nothing wrong—it had done exactly what it was supposed to do.

The 2016 Ukraine power grid attack served as a wake-up call to operators around the world. While DNP3 wasn't confirmed as the specific protocol targeted, the event highlighted the vulnerability of substation communications that assume trust and allow direct command execution. The attackers didn't need exploits—they needed access and fluency in the protocols. That blueprint could easily be adapted to a DNP3 environment, especially one using legacy configurations and flat networks.

That is the enduring dilemma of DNP3. It wasn't broken. It was obedient.

The path forward is not easy. Migration to Secure DNP3 requires investment, coordination, and in some cases, political capital. Vendors must support it consistently. Integrators must test it thoroughly. Operators must understand how to monitor and validate its performance. And security teams must recognize that protocol-level defense is only part of the solution. Network segmentation, anomaly detection, asset inventory, and human training all matter. DNP3 is only as secure as the environment it lives in.

What DNP3 illustrates—perhaps more clearly than any other protocol—is the danger of trusting assumptions that no longer hold. It was designed for trust, and that trust was once reasonable. But that world is gone. The serial line is now a fiber trunk. The private loop is now a routable subnet. And the engineer in the control room is now joined by a fleet of unmanaged devices, third-party contractors, and adversaries with time, tools, and motive.

In many ways, DNP3 is a victim of its own success. It worked so well, and for so long, that it became invisible. Its messages are small, its impact immense. And its vulnerabilities are quiet —until the moment they're not. Every time we route it across a wide-area network without secure wrappers, every time we leave port 20000 open to a field device, every time we assume the endpoint is unreachable or harmless, we are inviting risk into a space where consequence lives.

It is not enough to patch around the problem. It must be understood. DNP3 was built for performance, determinism, and cooperation. And in that world, it was beautiful. But in this one, it must be protected, compartmentalized, and scrutinized. Because it is still everywhere. And still listening.

CHAPTER 10 - PROFIBUS AND PROFINET: LEGACY IN THE LOOP

If Modbus is the protocol that wouldn't die, Profibus is the one that refuses to age—at least in the minds of its users. Born in the late 1980s as a fieldbus standard for process and manufacturing automation, Profibus emerged in Germany through a collaboration of government, academic, and industrial stakeholders. It was designed for robustness, deterministic timing, and vendor interoperability in an era when proprietary, closed-loop control systems dominated the landscape. It delivered on those promises. And because of that, it remains in service across hundreds of thousands of industrial facilities worldwide.

But Profibus was also built for a different time. Like many fieldbus protocols, it was optimized for real-time performance, not security. It assumed physical control equated to logical trust. It relied on tightly managed topologies, well-known devices, and the expectation that malicious interference was unlikely. What it never anticipated—what no one in that room in Karlsruhe could have predicted—was that its message formats would one day be traversing hybrid networks, relayed over Ethernet bridges, or exposed to IP-connected engineering stations controlled over VPN.

Profibus itself is simple and reliable. It operates over RS-485 and follows a master-slave model, with a single master controlling access to the bus and issuing requests to slave devices that respond in turn. This structure made it ideal for precise control applications where timing predictability mattered more than bandwidth or dynamic discovery. The Profibus DP variant, the most widely deployed, allows for fast data exchange with field devices like sensors and actuators. Profibus PA, meanwhile, supports intrinsically safe communication in process industries such as oil, gas, and chemicals.

From a protocol design standpoint, Profibus doesn't do authentication. It doesn't do encryption. It doesn't verify the integrity of messages beyond basic checksums. It lacks replay protection. Its trust model is physical: if you're on the wire, you're trusted. In closed, serial environments, this was arguably sufficient. But in many modern plants, Profibus is no longer confined to isolated wires. It has been integrated—often awkwardly—into broader IP-based networks, routed through protocol gateways and converted to Ethernet or TCP/IP traffic to accommodate converged control topologies. And in doing so, it has inherited all the risks of that convergence without gaining any of the protections.

Enter Profinet. Developed as the natural successor to Profibus, Profinet brought fieldbus semantics to Ethernet infrastructure. On paper, it solved many of Profibus's limitations. It supported faster data rates, greater scalability, and better integration with enterprise IT systems. It was modular, built with multiple communication classes—real-time, isochronous, and standard TCP/IP. Unlike Profibus, it allowed for richer device descriptions, standardized diagnostics, and dynamic configuration. But when it came to security, Profinet followed a now-familiar pattern: functionality first, threat modeling later.

At its core, Profinet relies on broadcast and multicast discovery. Devices announce themselves using Profinet Discovery and Configuration Protocol (DCP), a mechanism that allows engineering tools to locate, configure, and bind devices to specific control roles. This mechanism is fast, vendor-agnostic, and deterministic. It is also unauthenticated. Any device on the network can send DCP requests or respond to them. Any attacker with access to a mirrored port or compromised switch can issue forged responses, redirect configuration, or inject state changes. And because the protocol was designed for deterministic control, it often lacks the latency overhead required to implement TLS or complex challenge-response authentication.

In 2016, researchers demonstrated how trivial it was to exploit this trust. By spoofing Profinet DCP packets, an attacker could impersonate a device or redirect a controller's traffic to a rogue destination. In many configurations, this required no special privileges—just a presence on the network. The vulnerability wasn't a bug. It was a consequence of the protocol's design.

At a European packaging facility, a red-team simulation illustrated this in devastating clarity. The penetration testers began with access to a jump box inside the plant network. From there, they pivoted into a VLAN that included a Siemens SIMATIC S7-1500 PLC and several Profinet-connected actuators. Using freely available open-source tools, they passively captured DCP traffic, extracted MAC addresses and hostnames, and then crafted forged discovery packets. These impersonated the engineering workstation, which ran Siemens TIA Portal. By replying before the real device could respond, the rogue node tricked the TIA Portal into binding to it. From that point on, configuration commands and monitoring traffic were redirected to a counterfeit instance that mirrored normal behavior—while injecting subtle modifications to actuator timing. Conveyor speeds were altered by milliseconds, enough to cause downstream disruption without raising an alarm. There was no malware. No exploit. Just a design that trusted anything speaking Profinet.

Even where operators attempt to deploy resilience measures, the protocol's assumptions about trust bleed into its redundancy architecture. Profinet supports Media Redundancy Protocol and Parallel Redundancy Protocol to improve fault tolerance. These allow fast failover and dual-path communication, and they're often used in motion control and high-availability systems.

But neither protocol authenticates the frames they transmit. A malicious device can inject forged topology change notifications or duplicate frames to flood buffers or cause instability. The same mechanisms designed for safety and reliability can become conduits for attack if misconfigured or abused. That's the paradox at the heart of Profinet—what makes it reliable makes it fragile when placed in an untrusted context.

The broader issue isn't just Profinet's exposure—it's its ubiquity inside vendor-controlled ecosystems. Siemens, the principal developer and evangelist of both Profibus and Profinet, has engineered its automation environment to rely heavily on these protocols. From SIMATIC PLCs to engineering tools like TIA Portal, device discovery, status monitoring, and control flows are deeply entwined with protocol behavior. This tight coupling creates functional efficiency but introduces monoculture risk. Patching, monitoring, even segmentation design often hinges on proprietary knowledge. That opacity is a problem—not just for defenders trying to wrap controls around the protocol, but for integrators who want to add visibility without destabilizing performance.

To its credit, the PI consortium has proposed a security roadmap. Profinet Security Class 1 focuses on device hardening. Class 2 introduces cryptographic authentication for parameter access. Class 3 aims to support encrypted communication and session integrity. But most devices in the field predate these classifications, and even newer ones rarely ship with those capabilities enabled by default. Retrofits are complex. Real-time constraints limit handshake viability. And operators rarely have the resources to test and validate upgraded protocol stacks without triggering functional requalification. The intent is there. The path to adoption is not.

Profibus, though older, is far from gone. It remains deeply entrenched in process control, especially in brownfield plants where device lifespans are measured in decades. Many of these systems are still accessed via RS-485 serial links. But serial does not mean safe. In a mid-sized chemical processing facility in North America, a protocol converter had been installed to bridge a legacy Profibus segment with modern Ethernet-based SCADA. The converter allowed raw Profibus traffic to be forwarded over TCP/IP, exposing it to the broader OT network. The device had been deployed over ten years earlier, never updated, and its web configuration interface was accessible on the open subnet with no password. During a routine assessment, analysts discovered they could craft Profibus write commands via the converter's open port—changing polling frequencies, adjusting thresholds, and even disabling alarms. None of it was logged. No detection alerts were triggered. It had simply never occurred to anyone that Profibus, a cable-bound, deterministic protocol from the 1990s, might now be traversing a shared Ethernet backbone.

Defenders today rely on a patchwork of tools to see these protocols. Wireshark dissectors exist for both Profibus and Profinet, but are limited in depth and require manual parsing. Specialized monitoring platforms like Tenable OT, Claroty CTD, Nozomi Guardian, or open-source tools like GRASSMARLIN can detect and map industrial assets using Profinet signatures. But coverage is inconsistent, and many protocols are implemented with proprietary quirks that break parsers or evade detection altogether. What visibility exists is often the result of reverse engineering, not vendor support.

This opacity is made worse by the false confidence of certification. Many Profinet-based systems rely on safety-rated extensions like PROFIsafe, which ensure that faults are detected and that devices fail safely. But safety certification does not equal cybersecurity. A system certified to Safety Integrity Level 2 can still transmit those safety messages over an unauthenticated Profinet link. If the attacker can forge or replay them, the entire premise of system integrity collapses. Safety certification creates an illusion of control—but only if the transport layer is assumed to be trustworthy.

Profibus and Profinet are not inherently flawed. They were

designed for function, and they achieved it. But they now live in a world their designers never envisioned. A world of remote access, vendor APIs, hostile networks, and deeply skilled adversaries. What kept the line running yesterday may expose it tomorrow. And for all their mechanical simplicity, these protocols now operate within a digital terrain that punishes trust assumptions.

There is no single owner of this problem. Vendors must stop shipping insecure defaults and provide documented paths to secure deployment. Integrators must stop treating connectivity as configuration and begin validating trust boundaries. Operators must treat protocol management as a risk domain, not a maintenance task. Standards bodies must confront the reality that low-latency performance cannot justify plaintext messaging in critical infrastructure. Each party owns part of the problem. No one owns it entirely.

The future of Profibus and Profinet will not be defined by how well they worked in the past—but by how responsibly they are contained, compensated for, or replaced in the years to come. Because what was once a marvel of engineering may now be a liability. And in adversarial environments, trust is not a matter of tradition. It is a matter of design.

CHAPTER 11 - BROADCAST, DISCOVERY, AND THE ECHO CHAMBER

In the early days of local area networks, simplicity was the watchword. Networks were small, switches were few, and engineers often worked within the same room as the systems they maintained. Devices had to find each other with minimal configuration. It made sense, then, that many industrial protocols were built on a broadcast-first model: shout your presence to the entire network, and trust that the right recipient would hear you. What began as a convenience soon became a crutch, and over time, that crutch became a liability.

Broadcasts were never meant to scale. They were intended for simple topologies—flat, trusted networks where every node belonged. But the industrial world, like the IT world before it, didn't stay small. Buildings became campuses. Campuses became cities. Networks spanned continents. And yet many of the protocols that ran on them still operated under the assumption that if something was within earshot, it could be trusted. That assumption underpins protocols like BACnet, EtherNet/IP, PROFINET Discovery, and a host of vendor-specific implementations that were built for auto-detection, zero-configuration, and peer discovery across unmanaged networks.

BACnet is the quintessential example. Originally developed for building automation, it has become a foundational protocol for HVAC control, lighting systems, access control, and energy management. It was designed for ease of use. Devices broadcast their presence, announce available services, and identify peers automatically. Controllers discover sensors by listening. Lighting panels announce their state. Climate systems broadcast schedules. There is little formal authentication in most deployments, and often no segmentation. It just works—until it doesn't.

The problem with broadcast protocols is that they assume harmony. When devices are friendly, the echo chamber is functional. But introduce a rogue actor—intentional or accidental—and the same mechanisms become dangerous. A single device can flood the network with service announcements, triggering cascades of responses and overwhelming weaker nodes. An impersonated broadcast can convince a controller to route commands to the wrong endpoint. Misconfigured devices can rebroadcast messages endlessly, creating loops that saturate the subnet. In this environment, silence is rare and confusion is easy to manufacture.

Impersonation is trivial in many of these protocols because identity is tied to nothing more than MAC addresses, instance numbers, or broadcast headers. BACnet devices, for example, identify themselves using a simple device ID and instance number. If another device claims that ID, it becomes indistinguishable from the original in the eyes of most systems. There is no certificate chain, no mutual authentication, no cryptographic signature. It's a shouting match—and the loudest voice wins.

This lack of identity assurance leads to a class of attacks that are deceptively simple. A rogue device configured with the same instance ID as a legitimate controller can hijack messages, spoof status values, or silently discard commands. In some configurations, the controller won't know it has been deceived. Logs show success. Status lights remain green. But the field device is silent, disabled, or in the hands of the impersonator. This isn't a flaw in the protocol. It's an artifact of design assumptions rooted in trust and physical proximity—assumptions that no longer hold in converged environments.

Ethernet makes this problem worse. On flat networks, broadcast domains can span hundreds of devices and multiple switch hops. In smart building networks, where lighting, access control, elevators, and climate systems all live side by side, a single broadcast can ripple across the infrastructure and wake up devices that were never meant to interact. When an attacker floods a BACnet network with Who-Is requests—broadcast messages asking for all devices to identify themselves—the result can be hundreds of I-Am responses, each generating its own set of interactions, retries, and status updates. This is not just theoretical. In one red-team test, a well-timed Who-Is flood caused a campus-wide lighting controller to lose contact with half of its devices, triggering an overnight lighting reset and requiring manual re-pairing of every panel.

Many industrial networks still rely on Layer 2 switch architectures that offer minimal broadcast containment. In these environments, a single misconfigured node or broadcast storm can saturate uplinks, overwhelm switch buffers, and trigger cascading device failures—not from malicious intent, but from unfiltered volume. With unmanaged switches, there is often no storm control, no rate limiting, and no diagnostics. The network doesn't bend; it snaps. The protocol doesn't fail; the switch does.

Some protocols have attempted to sidestep the dangers of broadcast by adopting multicast instead—an approach that works only if the underlying network is configured to honor multicast group memberships. In practice, few industrial networks enable IGMP snooping or enforce proper group filtering. The result is that multicast traffic behaves like broadcast in all but name, traveling across entire subnets and awakening devices that were never meant to interact. Worse, when network gear misinterprets group joins or fails to prune dead paths, multicast floods become silent and persistent —consuming bandwidth and confusing operators without triggering alarms.

These attacks aren't loud in the traditional sense. They don't involve malformed packets or buffer overflows. They don't crash the devices with obvious exploits. They simply overload the ecosystem by leaning into its own communication habits. It is the equivalent of standing in a crowded room and shouting a question loud enough to get every person to respond at once— and then doing it again, and again, and again, until the room is no longer usable.

In more subtle cases, broadcast impersonation can be used to gather information rather than disrupt. A passive observer on a BACnet network can learn a great deal without sending a single packet. Devices advertise their function codes, firmware versions, and capabilities. Even if a device is not actively sending data, it may be listening for broadcasts that would trigger a response. By watching those interactions, a quiet attacker can fingerprint the network, map dependencies, and plan targeted disruption without ever tripping a single alarm.

Broadcast loops—unintentional or malicious—can be equally devastating. In smart buildings, misconfigured devices can rebroadcast each other's messages in an endless cycle. If two BACnet routers forward Who-Is messages across redundant paths, they may propagate endlessly between subnets. Without proper loop detection or rate limiting, the network becomes saturated. Performance degrades. Control signals are delayed or dropped. Devices fall out of sync. And in the worst cases, watchdog timers trigger system resets, pushing infrastructure into fail-safe or degraded states.

There's a persistent myth in building automation—that the broadcast domain is isolated, and thus harmless. But in practice, these networks are almost always connected to something else: a building management system, a vendor VPN, a cloud gateway, or a wireless bridge to a service room two floors down. That connection may not be obvious, but the broadcast traffic doesn't care. It crosses anyway. And so does anything listening. In one case, a tenant's home automation bridge in a mixed-use high-rise started forwarding mDNS and SSDP traffic into the building's BACnet VLAN. What followed wasn't a security breach, but a flood of device collisions and address resolution failures. The broadcast network wasn't air-gapped. It was porous —and vulnerable by design.

In converged networks, discovery traffic often includes mDNS, SSDP, and WS-Discovery—consumer-grade protocols used by everything from smart TVs to wireless printers. These systems operate with the same broadcast-first mindset as industrial protocols, but they're even noisier. A single Apple device can flood the network with Bonjour announcements. A misconfigured media server can blast SSDP packets to every IP it can see. In shared infrastructure, these messages cross paths with BACnet, LLDP, and EtherNet/IP—creating a soup of discovery traffic that overwhelms logging tools and masks real signals in the noise.

Real-world cases illustrate just how subtle and impactful these dynamics can be. In one international airport, a vendor misconfigured a new HVAC controller that issued repeated BACnet broadcast queries without properly caching responses. Each time it was powered on, it asked for all devices to identify themselves—every few seconds. The resulting flood didn't crash the network, but it introduced just enough delay that air handlers periodically failed to update their setpoints, causing climate drift in passenger areas and escalating into a service ticket backlog. It took weeks to trace the issue to the root cause, not because it was technically complex, but because no one suspected a discovery protocol could do that much damage.

In large industrial campuses, the issue becomes one of scale. As more devices are added to the network—smart meters, access panels, occupancy sensors—the broadcast surface grows. Each new node increases the number of recipients for each message, and each recipient may trigger its own chatter in response. Without aggressive segmentation and VLAN enforcement, discovery messages traverse the entire environment. What was once a quiet subnet becomes a crowded echo chamber, full of devices shouting and responding with no memory of who spoke first.

Broadcast-based discovery protocols also serve as reconnaissance channels for adversaries. Tools like BACnet-Scan and Project Bacnet have made it easy for attackers and researchers alike to discover and interact with exposed BACnet devices across the public internet. In some scans, BACnet-speaking devices have been found broadcasting services over WAN links, either due to misconfiguration or deliberate exposure. These systems often include HVAC controllers, lighting panels, or access systems in smart buildings—deployed without firewall rules or VPNs, and speaking openly to anyone who asks.

Discovery protocols are also prone to amplification. A carefully crafted Who-Is packet sent to dozens of BACnet devices can generate hundreds of I-Am responses—each larger than the original query. When these messages are spoofed with a forged source IP, they can be used as part of a reflective DDoS attack. While not as volumetric as NTP or DNS amplification, the technique has been observed in targeted attacks against building management networks, especially those exposed to the internet due to misconfigured routers or legacy vendor installs.

Broadcast-heavy environments don't just respond to probes—they call out to anyone listening. For a patient adversary who has compromised a single foothold inside a network, these broadcasts become beacons. Without scanning, they learn what systems are present, what firmware they run, what vendor software is in use, and what topology governs the environment. Discovery traffic leaks metadata constantly, and no alarm is triggered when it does. In that silence, the adversary gains the advantage—not by sending anything, but by listening to a conversation that was never meant to be private.

The impersonation risk goes beyond BACnet. Protocols like LLDP (Link Layer Discovery Protocol), used in Ethernet infrastructure for topology awareness, also operate via broadcast. LLDP packets are accepted without challenge and can be spoofed by any device. In certain configurations, a malicious LLDP broadcast can convince a switch to reconfigure port settings or trigger VLAN changes—leading to unexpected bridging or segmentation failures. Similarly, EtherNet/IP, PROFINET, and other industrial Ethernet variants include discovery mechanisms that are trivially spoofable, often relying on MAC address binding or unvalidated session IDs.

Some of the most disruptive broadcast behaviors come not from standardized protocols but from vendor-specific additions. Custom discovery protocols embedded in firmware update tools, license managers, or proprietary configuration software may broadcast on irregular intervals or undocumented ports. These "stealth broadcasts" often go unnoticed until they trigger unexpected congestion. Worse, because they are undocumented, standard monitoring tools ignore them— leaving engineers with a symptom and no root cause. In one case, a third-party elevator monitoring system quietly broadcasted beacon packets every two seconds across an entire subnet. No alarms were triggered, but the switch eventually failed under the weight of invisible noise.

In converged environments, where IT and OT share infrastructure, these discovery echoes become dangerous in new ways. IT staff may deploy intrusion prevention systems or port-security mechanisms that respond aggressively to unexpected traffic. A sudden burst of BACnet discovery packets may be interpreted as a scan or attack, triggering automated shutdowns. Conversely, OT staff may be unaware that their trusted protocols are flooding switches with traffic the IT side was never meant to see. In these scenarios, neither side is wrong

—but both are surprised.

What makes this even more challenging is that discovery protocols are often undocumented in asset inventories. When a device is added to the network, its primary function is logged—the fact that it speaks BACnet or LLDP is not. So when it begins flooding the network, no one knows where to look. The response is reactive, manual, and often disruptive. In one manufacturing plant, a technician installed a new access controller that used BACnet to advertise itself. The device behaved normally in the lab, but on the production floor, it was placed behind a switch that had storm control disabled. Within hours, latency began to increase across the control network. PLCs lost synchronization. HMI refresh rates dropped. And yet, the controller continued to function. No one suspected it because it hadn't failed—it had just spoken too loudly in the wrong room.

Defense against broadcast abuse is conceptually simple but operationally difficult. The first step is segmentation. Broadcast domains must be small, deliberate, and isolated by function. BACnet devices should not share a subnet with security cameras, access panels, or IT infrastructure. Discovery traffic should be throttled, rate-limited, and monitored. VLAN boundaries should be enforced not just by switch configuration but by policy. Routers and firewalls should block or log broadcast requests crossing zone boundaries. These are not expensive controls—but they require coordination, planning, and political capital between departments that may not share goals or language.

More advanced defenses involve protocol-aware monitoring. Tools that understand BACnet or LLDP can identify anomalous behavior—floods, impersonation, or response storms—and alert without relying on traditional signatures. But few organizations deploy these tools broadly, and even fewer tune them to reflect real operational conditions. As with so much in OT, visibility is the first challenge. If you can't see it, you can't defend it.

Discovery protocols aren't inherently flawed. They serve a purpose—especially in dynamic or temporary environments like commissioning, diagnostics, or rapidly evolving facilities. But they must be contained. Their presence should be temporary, their scope defined, and their behavior observable. Like fire inside a furnace, broadcast traffic can be productive—but only if it is controlled, directed, and denied the chance to spread.

Ultimately, the danger of broadcast-heavy protocols is not in the protocols themselves. It is in their scale, their default behaviors, and the silence that surrounds them. When a discovery mechanism works too well, it becomes a magnet for misuse. When it works silently, it becomes invisible. And when it works trustingly, it becomes dangerous. Broadcasts are meant to help devices find each other. But in the echo chamber of a modern industrial network, they can just as easily help adversaries find you.

And once they do, they don't need to break in. They just need to speak up—and listen for the answers.

CHAPTER 12 - CIP AND THE MYTH OF INDUSTRIAL INTEROPERABILITY

For a protocol that set out to unify industrial communication, the Common Industrial Protocol did more than standardize—it defined an entire ecosystem. Built by Rockwell Automation and stewarded by the Open DeviceNet Vendors Association, CIP was intended to be vendor-neutral, modular, and scalable across multiple physical and transport layers. It succeeded in those goals, at least from a functionality standpoint. Today, CIP is embedded in the DNA of many automation environments, especially in North America. From the serial legacy of DeviceNet to the Ethernet efficiency of EtherNet/IP, CIP has become the lingua franca of Allen-Bradley systems and a pillar of automotive, pharmaceutical, and discrete manufacturing sectors.

But like so many industrial protocols, CIP was never designed for security. Its abstraction model, transport behavior, and communication assumptions reflect a time before convergence, before remote access, before the idea that control traffic might need to defend itself. The elegance of its object-oriented structure masks a troubling truth: CIP speaks freely, trusts deeply, and authenticates almost nothing. Its greatest virtue—interoperability—has become its most exploitable flaw.

At its core, CIP defines a rich object model where each device is a collection of predefined classes—Identity, Assembly,

Connection, Analog Input—and each class exposes attributes and services. These are further refined into application-specific profiles. A variable frequency drive, for instance, will expose a predictable combination of CIP objects tied to its operational state. These profiles were designed for interoperability, allowing devices from different vendors to be swapped or monitored with minimal reconfiguration. But the same predictability also creates a blueprint for attackers. Once a device is identified, its application profile suggests exactly which services it will respond to, which objects are critical to operation, and what assumptions its PLC scanner is likely making.

Communication happens via service codes sent to these objects, encapsulated in a messaging layer defined by the CIP specification. Whether the transport is serial (as in DeviceNet), deterministic coaxial (as in ControlNet), or Ethernet (as in EtherNet/IP), the message structure remains the same. This architectural consistency made it easy to extend and support across devices. But it also means that vulnerabilities in how services are exposed or invoked tend to propagate across implementations.

CIP messaging is categorized as either implicit or explicit. Implicit messaging is time-sensitive, cyclic I/O traffic—used for real-time control between PLCs and field devices. It typically runs over UDP, using multicast for distribution. Explicit messaging handles configuration, diagnostics, and less frequent interactions. These messages ride over TCP and include the familiar Get_Attribute, Set_Attribute, and Unconnected_Send service codes. The combination of real-time speed and rich query support made CIP attractive for integrators—but also for adversaries.

CIP's multicast behavior introduces fragility at scale. Many networks allow multicast packets to propagate without IGMP snooping or router control-plane restrictions. As a result, a single device sending cyclic traffic to a group address can cause that traffic to flood switch uplinks, overwhelm field devices, or disrupt HMI communications. In several factory environments, denial-of-service events have been traced not to malicious intent, but to misconfigured IGMP queriers or overlapping address ranges among CIP multicast groups. But once attackers understand this behavior, they can replicate it deliberately. A single forged multicast stream with spoofed MAC addresses can degrade plant communications without ever touching a PLC directly.

CIP's object structure is inherently enumerable. Anyone who can send a Get_Attribute_All request to the Identity object can extract the device's name, vendor ID, product type, revision number, and more. From there, more targeted requests can explore other objects: what sensors are present, how many connections are allowed, what services are implemented. In modern networks, this often means that an attacker can identify not just the presence of a Rockwell device, but its model, firmware version, and configuration parameters within seconds of accessing a flat subnet. No authentication is required. No rate limiting is enforced. CIP was designed for trust—designed to allow tools like RSLogix and Studio 5000 to rapidly scan and configure devices on the fly. But when that trust is violated, the result is silent, precise reconnaissance.

That reconnaissance becomes even more powerful once the attacker understands CIP's Scanner/Adapter model. In EtherNet/IP, the Scanner is the controller—usually a PLC or PAC—that initiates communication and manages session state. Adapters are field devices—drives, sensors, relays—that respond to scan requests and provide data. But nothing prevents a rogue Scanner from broadcasting a request to every Adapter in a network. There's no cryptographic binding between Scanner and Adapter. If the message matches the expected class and instance, it is accepted. In several red-team engagements, attackers introduced counterfeit Scanners that assumed control of devices mid-process, overriding expected setpoints or halting production without any alarms. The control plane itself never questioned the change.

In one simulation conducted inside a bottling plant, testers connected to a span port inside a supposedly isolated VLAN. Within minutes, using standard libraries and a packet capture tool, they had fingerprinted every EtherNet/IP-capable PLC on the network. Each one responded to queries. Each one exposed its identity, configuration, and connection parameters. And each one could have been targeted for disruption—not through exploits, but through protocol-native behavior. In a follow-up test, a rogue Scanner was introduced to the subnet. Because the field devices accepted new connection requests without validation, the counterfeit controller began sending cyclic updates that conflicted with the original control logic. There was no alert. The real controller simply lost arbitration and was ignored.

For all its openness and lack of native defenses, CIP paradoxically offers defenders some of the richest telemetry available in industrial networks. Its object-oriented architecture exposes a granular view of device state, from identity information to connection tables, I/O assembly mappings, diagnostic registers, and session statistics. This structure, which attackers use for reconnaissance, can also serve as a foundation for real-time asset intelligence—if defenders have the tools and access to use it properly.

Platforms like Tenable OT, Claroty CTD, Nozomi Guardian, and Cisco Cyber Vision are increasingly capable of parsing CIP traffic passively, mapping out Scanner-to-Adapter relationships, monitoring session durations, flagging changes in implicit I/O frequency, and even alerting on suspicious or unauthorized use of service codes like Unconnected_Send or Get_Attribute_All. These systems don't rely on device agents. Instead, they observe the protocol's native behavior on the wire, building baselines and highlighting deviations. They can identify when a new Scanner comes online, when a device changes state unexpectedly, or when cyclic traffic suddenly drops from a known participant. In networks with flat addressing and limited documentation, this level of introspection offers critical situational awareness that traditional IT security tools can't provide.

Tenable OT Security takes this a step further by integrating CIP-based insights with vulnerability intelligence. Through its passive inspection and active fingerprinting modules, it can identify the exact model and firmware version of Rockwell devices, correlate them with known CVEs, and generate tailored risk scores. It can determine whether a device is exposing unauthenticated services, whether it supports CIP Security but has it disabled, and whether its BootP/DHCP server is still active on the subnet. This moves CIP beyond diagnostics and into risk quantification. What was once simply object metadata becomes a lens into lifecycle state, exposure posture, and potential exploitability.

The problem, then, is not that CIP hides too much—it's that it shares indiscriminately. Every device speaks openly to anyone who asks, under the assumption that every request is made in good faith. But if that same transparency is scoped, authenticated, and integrated into security operations, CIP can become one of the most powerful sources of context-aware telemetry in the industrial stack. Its structure lends itself to monitoring. Its verbosity can be a feature. But only if those doing the monitoring understand what they're looking at—and only if the environment has been architected to trust selectively, not universally.

What makes this more dangerous is that many CIP deployments rely on insecure auxiliary services. Rockwell BootP/DHCP tools, for example, are widely used to assign static IP addresses to new PLCs or I/O modules during commissioning. These services typically operate on broadcast networks with no authentication. In some plants, they remain active indefinitely—even after commissioning ends. An attacker who impersonates a BootP server can reassign device IPs, redirect traffic, or force devices to reboot by supplying malformed responses. This vulnerability isn't theoretical—it's been exploited in live environments where teams left default utilities running "just in case" they needed to reconfigure something quickly.

To address these issues, ODVA introduced a specification called CIP Security. It includes support for TLS-based encryption, secure session establishment, and authorization of service access based on roles. On paper, it's a comprehensive solution. But in the field, its deployment remains rare. CIP Security requires not only firmware support but proper key management, certificate provisioning, and changes to the control logic that may impact timing and performance. For real-time I/O, many vendors have opted to leave CIP Security disabled, fearing it might introduce jitter or connection instability. The result is a protocol with a modern spec but an insecure footprint. Secure by design, but insecure by default.

Even as some defenders try to harden CIP with segmentation and inspection, the trend toward cloud-based monitoring and IIoT visibility compounds the risk. Increasingly, EtherNet/IP traffic is routed through edge gateways, translated into MQTT or REST APIs, and sent to cloud dashboards for predictive analytics. These gateways often strip context, sanitize payloads, or reduce field data to metrics—losing the session semantics and object integrity of the original CIP messages. If the translation layer is compromised or misconfigured, attackers can alter control state through a side channel while bypassing traditional detection mechanisms. In one case study, a cloud-connected CIP gateway accepted OTA updates via HTTPS but failed to validate the firmware signature. Once compromised, the gateway served as both eavesdropper and bridge, quietly relaying falsified CIP messages into the plant's internal network.

CIP has become one of the most well-documented and freely accessible industrial protocols. Open source libraries like pycomm3, cpppo, and EIPScanner allow anyone with basic Python skills to query devices, extract attributes, or send crafted service requests. Vendors have embraced CIP's ease of use by building thin clients and web APIs that rely on its service architecture. But ease cuts both ways. The very transparency that makes integration simple makes exploitation easier. And when that exploitation happens, it often occurs invisibly. Many PLCs do not log failed service requests. Most do not alert on unauthorized reads. And few have any built-in concept of anomalous behavior detection.

The danger is amplified by the myth of safety. Many CIP-based devices are certified for functional safety—SIL-2 or SIL-3 performance under fault conditions. These ratings often come through the use of protocols like CIP Safety, which implements redundant, timed, CRC-protected messages across a known-good channel. But that channel is often the same one used by unauthenticated TCP or UDP traffic. The assumption is that the network is clean, the participants are known, and the timing is predictable. Once those assumptions collapse, the safety rating does too. Safety is not a substitute for security, and CIP's safety mechanisms do not prevent a compromised device from issuing valid but malicious instructions.

The irony of CIP is that it fulfilled its goal. It brought structure to a fragmented protocol landscape. It enabled vendor interoperability, object standardization, and reusable device profiles. But the more it unified, the more it exposed. CIP made integration easier, but it also made attack surfaces uniform. It made diagnostics transparent, but it also made reconnaissance trivial. In a world where anyone could be a threat actor, CIP assumed that no one would be.

CIP still powers much of industrial America. But if the industry wants to keep that infrastructure from becoming a liability, it must stop assuming that compatibility is protection. Interoperability is not security. It is simply communication. And communication without verification is no longer a neutral act—it is an open invitation.

The way forward will require uncomfortable decisions and a disciplined approach to containment. No protocol this open can ever be fully secured in the traditional sense—but it can be constrained, monitored, and governed with the seriousness its risks demand. That begins with containing exposure. CIP devices must be isolated behind segmented networks, with multicast scoped by IGMP controls and access lists that restrict who can initiate Scanner behavior. Unused services—like BootP, web consoles, or legacy HTTP interfaces—must be shut down. These aren't conveniences anymore. They're attack surfaces.

Where newer devices support CIP Security, it must be enabled, even at the cost of minor complexity. TLS-based session encryption and role-based service access are not theoretical upgrades—they are now requirements. For older systems where that's not feasible, the fallback is control: define trusted Scanner-Adapter relationships and alert on any deviation from them. Unauthorized queries should be treated as reconnaissance. Unrecognized scanners should trigger incident response. There is no legitimate reason for a rogue PLC to initiate a cyclic stream on a Saturday afternoon.

Defenders should use CIP's verbosity to their advantage. Passive inspection tools like Claroty, Nozomi, Cisco Cyber Vision, and Tenable OT can extract the full shape of the network from on-the-wire behavior, mapping Scanner-Adapter relationships, detecting unauthorized use of service codes, and flagging changes in session frequency. But beyond passive monitoring, active inspection—when performed deliberately and with appropriate safety controls—can yield even richer visibility. Tools, like Tenable OT, that query device identity objects, poll for connection parameters, or read assembly configurations over authenticated sessions can surface vulnerabilities, deviations from expected state, or even unpatched firmware versions. Done right, this kind of active polling mimics the behavior of trusted engineering tools and can be integrated into scheduled security assessments without disrupting plant operations. In these environments, CIP isn't just a control channel—it's a forensic trail. And if that trail is parsed intelligently, it becomes one of the most powerful early warning systems defenders have.

That same structure also allows for auditing. Every CIP device exposes its configuration in the open. From I/O assembly instances to timeout parameters to object class mappings, defenders can validate control logic assumptions against live behavior. Changes here are often a precursor to manipulation. Regular audits—whether via protocol-aware tools or authenticated polling—can catch drift before it turns into compromise.

If the plant is using edge gateways to route data into the cloud, then those gateways must become security choke points. They must verify firmware signatures, enforce TLS, and preserve protocol context during translation. A cloud dashboard that shows metrics without verifying the origin of control messages isn't just blind—it's dangerous.

And finally, operators must stop assuming that safety equates to security. CIP Safety may guarantee message fidelity within a bounded context, but it cannot protect against a rogue Scanner issuing valid commands outside that context. If the transport layer is untrusted, the safety claim collapses under the weight of its own assumptions.

This isn't a call for protocol perfection. It's a blueprint for realistic defense. Harden what you can. Monitor what you can't. Control what you must. And never trust a protocol to protect what its designers never imagined could be at risk.

CHAPTER 13 – BROADCAST AND OBEY: BACNET AND THE INSECURITY OF SMART BUILDINGS

The elevator doors opened into an empty lobby. A row of motion sensors, embedded in ceiling tiles, silently registered the entry. Temperature sensors adjusted the airflow from a variable air volume system to match occupancy expectations. Overhead lights brightened in response to scheduled timing profiles, and an HVAC controller on the eighth floor began adjusting the humidity settings for a conference room in preparation for a board meeting. None of this behavior was coordinated by a human. It was BACnet—unseen, unauthenticated, and obedient.

In that same building, an attacker with a laptop could walk in, plug into an exposed Ethernet port labeled "Security Room Access," and with two or three broadcast packets, enumerate the entire automation system. In under a minute, they could identify every thermostat, occupancy sensor, elevator control module, fan coil, and door lock. In five minutes, they could issue write commands to shut off cooling, trigger false alarms, or unlock restricted areas. There would be no passwords to bypass. No access tokens to forge. The network would respond because BACnet does not ask why. It simply listens. And when asked, it obeys.

BACnet—short for Building Automation and Control Network

—was developed in the late 1980s by ASHRAE (the American Society of Heating, Refrigerating and Air-Conditioning Engineers). Its design reflected the practical needs of building engineers and facility managers: a vendor-neutral protocol that could coordinate HVAC, lighting, fire detection, and access control across devices from different manufacturers. At a time when proprietary control protocols locked customers into single-vendor ecosystems, BACnet offered freedom through interoperability. It succeeded wildly in that mission. By the early 2000s, it had become the dominant standard in building automation, adopted globally across commercial real estate, hospitals, airports, data centers, and government facilities. But that interoperability came with a price.

The core of BACnet's behavior is trust—implicit, automatic, and complete. Devices announce themselves on the network with "I-Am" packets. Controllers discover peers with "Who-Is" requests. Properties—both read-only and writable—are exposed without credentials. The philosophy was simple: if a device is connected to the network, it is authorized to participate. There was no threat model. No adversaries assumed. The building was a safe space.

As long as these systems remained isolated—segregated from IT networks, limited to serial lines or controlled subnets—the risk was manageable. But like other OT protocols, BACnet made the leap to IP. BACnet/IP became the standard, and with it came the shift to Ethernet switches, routed networks, and shared infrastructure. BACnet traffic began appearing on the same cables that carried business operations, video surveillance, and in some cases, internet access. And once that happened, the assumptions that had protected it collapsed.

In red team exercises, BACnet is often the fastest path to tangible impact. It does not require privilege escalation. It does not require lateral movement in the traditional sense. All that is needed is visibility into the broadcast domain. From there, everything opens up. The devices identify themselves, describe their functions, expose their writable properties, and accept control commands from any node that speaks the protocol. In one such engagement, an attacker spoofed the identity of a BACnet supervisory controller and issued a global command to disable VAV dampers across three floors of an office tower. The result was temperature spikes, panic calls to facilities, and a half-day investigation into what appeared to be a cascade failure. No malware was used. No exploit was triggered. The attacker had simply joined the conversation.

These incidents are not hypothetical. Public demonstrations at conferences like DEF CON have shown how tools like YABE and BACnet-Scapy can be used to map and control an entire building with minimal effort. MITRE's Project SIEVE went further, demonstrating how adversaries could exploit BACnet objects to alter building behavior in ways that directly affected safety and availability. In academic research, BACnet has been labeled a "broadcast protocol with control authority"—a phrase that should terrify anyone managing modern infrastructure.

The idea that BACnet controls "only HVAC" is a dangerous misconception. A typical building automation system includes integration with fire detection zones, smoke evacuation systems, access card readers, smart lighting controllers, elevator dispatch logic, and generator start/stop relays. In data centers and hospitals, BACnet is often directly linked to environmental control systems whose failure could affect uptime guarantees, medical storage integrity, or patient safety. A malicious or malformed command in these environments doesn't just create discomfort—it can trigger real-world harm.

Compounding this exposure is the fragmented and risk-indifferent vendor ecosystem that surrounds BACnet devices. Many vendors ship devices with BACnet/IP enabled by default, listening on UDP port 47808 with no authentication. Default object IDs are reused across deployments, enabling attackers to identify device functions even without full enumeration. Web interfaces often wrap around BACnet functionality, exposing control objects through unauthenticated HTTP or even cloud-linked dashboards. In some cases, vendors offer no way to disable BACnet features—even if the device is being deployed in a high-security environment. The notion of least privilege is completely absent from the protocol's implementation.

These vulnerabilities are compounded when BACnet devices are exposed to the internet. Shodan queries reveal hundreds—sometimes thousands—of internet-facing BACnet devices at any given time, many of them tied to critical or high-profile facilities. Public school districts, universities, municipal buildings, and even airports have appeared in scans. Often these exposures result from misconfigured cloud gateways or integration platforms that bridge local automation networks to remote analytics providers. The devices were never intended to be directly reachable. But reachability is what modern connectivity delivers by default.

BACnet/SC—Secure Connect—was introduced to fix this. It replaces broadcast-based discovery with TLS-encrypted communications, certificate-based identity verification, and point-to-point trusted sessions. Conceptually, it offers real security: no more unauthenticated write commands, no more open broadcasting, no more silent eavesdropping on system behavior. But adoption has been tepid. Most vendors have yet to ship full BACnet/SC implementations, and those that do often require costly firmware upgrades or controller replacements. The migration path is complex, often requiring new key management infrastructure, updated tooling, and retraining for integration teams. Most critically, BACnet/SC breaks the assumption of effortless plug-and-play. It demands planning. It adds friction. And in the world of building integration, friction is often treated as an operational failure.

As a result, nearly all deployed BACnet systems still operate over BACnet/IP, using UDP broadcasts and trusting every packet they receive.

Defenders attempt to compensate. VLAN segmentation, firewalled subnets, and protocol-aware gateways help reduce exposure. But these mitigations are brittle. A misconfigured switch port, an overlooked engineering laptop, a VPN concentrator with split-tunneling enabled—any one of these creates a pathway back into the broadcast domain. And once there, the protocol will behave as it always has: listening, announcing, responding.

Compromise isn't limited to digital abuse. In a recent case study, a red teamer gained access to a BACnet network not by scanning or phishing, but by posing as HVAC support. Wearing a uniform shirt and carrying a clipboard, the attacker entered a mechanical room under the pretext of scheduled diagnostics. Inside, they connected a small single-board computer with a BACnet stack to an open wall jack labeled "RTU Primary," configured it for promiscuous broadcast listening, and left. Over the next 72 hours, the device collected topology information, enumerated writable objects, and mapped the building's automation system. No alarms were triggered. No network defenses flagged the presence of a new device. And because the traffic looked like standard BACnet behavior, no one thought to investigate.

This is the quiet reality of BACnet abuse: attackers do not need to break in. They need only to blend in. The protocol does not distinguish between inquiry and intrusion. It trusts the source. It trusts the intent. And it exposes the building's digital nervous system to anyone fluent in its language.

Defending against BACnet threats requires a shift in how buildings are understood—not as passive structures, but as cyber-physical ecosystems with control surfaces as vulnerable as any firewall or database. Building management systems must be inventoried, mapped, and monitored like the critical infrastructure they are. BACnet traffic should be baselined, inspected, and constrained. Writable object commands should be logged. Protocol-aware firewalls must understand the structure of BACnet messages and enforce rules at the object and function level—not just IP and port.

Above all, organizations must break the cultural perception that building systems are exempt from security scrutiny. A thermostat that listens to unverified commands is no less dangerous than a file server with anonymous write access. A controller that adjusts ventilation based on broadcast messages is no less vulnerable than a web application with unsanitized inputs.

BACnet was designed for a world without adversaries. That world no longer exists. And while new protocols promise better futures, most buildings still run on trust. Trust in the broadcast. Trust in the packet. Trust in the silence between alarms.

But trust, as this book has repeatedly shown, is a liability in disguise.

CHAPTER 14 - THE SIEMENS STACK: S7, GATEWAYS, AND THE LEGACY OF TRUST

The Siemens S7 protocol was never meant to be public. Like many industrial protocols born in the 1990s, it was built for function, performance, and interoperability—within an ecosystem that was never supposed to touch the internet. Developed as the internal communications language for SIMATIC S7 PLCs, the protocol enabled seamless integration with engineering tools such as STEP 7 and later TIA Portal. It allowed engineers to read and write memory blocks, control logic flows, and perform online diagnostics without barriers. What made it powerful for operations, however, also rendered it dangerously exposed in an age when networks are adversarial. S7 operates over ISO-on-TCP on port 102 without cryptographic handshakes, challenge–response, or session verification; it assumes that any client initiating a connection is inherently trusted. There are no credentials, no integrity checks, and no provisions to challenge malicious usage. The protocol simply accepts structured commands—read, write, control, upload, download—as long as the device is listening, based solely on the presumption that physical proximity ensured trust. In today's converged and dynamic networks, that assumption is no longer valid.

For years, the inner workings of S7 were undocumented and proprietary. Then, following the revelation of Stuxnet, reverse-engineering efforts through projects like Snap7, Libnodave, and

S7Comm Wireshark dissectors opened the protocol to the world —democratizing not only integration but also exploitation. With only a packet capture and an IP address, attackers learned they could discover Siemens PLCs, interrogate their status, extract running logic, and even overwrite memory via protocol-native messages without any form of authentication.

Stuxnet's emergence in 2010 was a watershed moment that underscored S7's inherent insecurity. Developed by nation-state actors, Stuxnet targeted Siemens S7-300 and S7-400 series PLCs in uranium enrichment facilities at Natanz. It did not rely on a single zero-day or a novel exploit of the S7 protocol itself. Instead, it exploited weaknesses in the Windows environment —beginning with a zero-day in Windows shortcut file parsing that executed code merely by viewing an infected USB drive. From there, the malware leveraged additional vulnerabilities in the print spooler, RPC handling, and task scheduling. It chained these exploits to escalate privileges and move laterally within the network, eventually bypassing the defenses of engineering workstations. Once inside, Stuxnet masqueraded as legitimate STEP 7 software, injecting carefully crafted code into targeted memory blocks using native S7 instructions. The PLC logic continued to function—but with subtle, hidden alterations that gradually modified process timing and induced material fatigue, all while operator consoles remained unaware and alarms stayed silent. The protocol did not resist; it simply obeyed.

That attack highlighted that S7 was never designed for an environment where adversaries might deliberately subvert trust. It was built for isolated control rooms and direct physical access, not for networks where devices communicate across firewalls and even into the cloud. Yet today, the Siemens environment has evolved, and with it, the role of gateways has become critical. S7 Gateways, which bridge disparate network segments and route traffic from engineering workstations to PLCs, act as the essential intermediaries in many plants. They often connect multiple zones—between the control network and the enterprise—without sufficiently isolating or logging the messages they forward. As such, these gateways present a twofold vulnerability: they not only expose the inherent trust of the S7 protocol by aggregating control traffic but also become single points of failure that, if compromised, allow attackers to manipulate or obscure the true operational status of the connected devices.

A 2018 penetration test at a packaging plant illustrated the danger vividly. Red-team operators discovered a Siemens Gateway PC running outdated Windows XP that bridged both the engineering VLAN and the control network. This gateway, running WinCC for HMI visualization and serving as the primary conduit for STEP 7 communication, was exploited via a known SMB vulnerability. Once inside, the attackers used Snap7 to impersonate a TIA Portal workstation, extracting live PLC memory, mapping the program logic, and subtly injecting modifications into the control timers. The operator interface continued to show normal conditions, yet the production process began to drift, destabilized by gradual, undetected changes. In that instance, the gateway had become an effective proxy for the attacker, compromising the integrity of the entire control system without any alarms being raised.

Even without explicit attacks like that, the very nature of gateways creates severe challenges for monitoring and defense. Many gateways perform protocol translation, bridging the gap between Ethernet and serial communications. This encapsulation often strips away the original source information, leaving monitoring systems with only an aggregated view of the network—the gateway's version of events rather than the raw data from the PLCs. In many designs, monitoring tools are deployed upstream of the gateway, meaning that the only information available is what the gateway chooses to expose through diagnostics, SNMP data, or its proprietary API. This scenario forces defenders to place blind trust in the gateway's reporting. If the gateway has been compromised or misconfigured, its data may be outdated, incomplete, or even deliberately falsified, giving the attacker a stealthy channel to manipulate communications unseen. Even active scanning, intended to fill this gap, can be rendered ineffective if the gateway blocks or rewrites polling requests. Consequently, the gateway becomes a single point of trust—a soft perimeter that, if exploited, undermines any visibility into the actual field devices.

Beyond these architectural challenges, defenders must contend with broader issues inherent in legacy environments. Continuous asset inventory and proactive vulnerability management become essential, as many Siemens systems have been in place for decades. In a modern plant, the challenge is not simply to secure a freshly deployed system; it is to maintain and monitor hardware that may be well past its intended operational life. Organizations must adopt processes that continuously map every asset, flag firmware mismatches, and correlate any changes against a backdrop of emerging threat intelligence. Platforms like Tenable OT can integrate with CIP data to fingerprint devices accurately, match them with known vulnerabilities, and generate risk scores that are updated in real time. Such proactive measures are critical to turn static legacy networks into agile, resilient environments, even if only incrementally.

These technical challenges are compounded by economic and cultural inertia. Operators in industries that have relied on Siemens hardware for decades face enormous hurdles when contemplating upgrades. The cost of replacing a PLC, retraining staff, or navigating recertification processes can be prohibitive. As a result, many organizations become locked into maintaining systems that "just work" despite their inherent vulnerabilities. The human factor is just as critical as the technical, as seasoned engineers may resist changes that disrupt familiar workflows—even when those workflows are built on decades-old, insecure protocols. Without strong leadership willing to invest in modernization and enforce rigorous security policies, the vulnerabilities inherent in S7 and its gateways will persist.

Regulatory frameworks and industry standards offer some hope but often fall short of transformative change. Standards such as IEC 62443 provide guidelines for protecting industrial control systems through segmentation, risk assessment, and secure maintenance. However, many plants operate on technology that predates these modern standards, and compliance often becomes a checkbox exercise rather than a catalyst for proactive security. The disconnect between certification and operational reality further emphasizes the need for continuous monitoring, vulnerability management, and a cultural shift towards aggressive risk mitigation.

Despite these hurdles, there are success stories that highlight a path forward. In one instance, an industrial facility integrated Tenable OT with platforms like Claroty and Nozomi to establish a continuous, real-time inventory of its Siemens devices. When the system flagged an unexpected deviation in a PLC's I/O assembly mapping, the security team was alerted immediately. Further investigation revealed that a misconfigured gateway was inadvertently routing traffic from a decommissioned controller to an active PLC. This incident was remediated quickly because proactive visibility and integrated threat intelligence had been established. In another example, an automotive plant overhauled its asset management protocols by deploying automated tools that continuously updated its Siemens stack inventory. Not only did this approach identify unpatched firmware and unauthorized devices, it also built a compelling business case for gradual modernization, despite significant upfront costs.

The broader lesson is not that S7 is irredeemable, but that it was designed under assumptions that no longer apply. Its transparency, extensibility, and efficiency are still valuable, but in an era of pervasive cyber threats, they turn into liabilities without layered defenses. To secure the Siemens stack, defenders must rethink the architecture rather than expect the protocol itself to be secure. This means hardening engineering workstations through strict access controls and continuous logging, rigorously segmenting networks so that gateways become controlled intersections rather than open bridges, and deploying both passive and active monitoring systems that can continuously correlate asset inventory, vulnerability data, and threat intelligence. When a gateway is the only portal into a sensitive zone, its integrity must be ensured through hardened configurations and comprehensive audit trails.

The future of Siemens stack security depends on a multifaceted approach. Vendors must commit to shipping secure defaults and enable technologies like S7Comm+ where possible. Operators must invest in continuous monitoring and vulnerability management programs that keep legacy devices in check. Integrators must design networks with strict segmentation and enforce robust authentication in every communication channel. And regulatory bodies must bridge the gap between aspirational standards and operational practices, ensuring that even legacy environments are not left defenseless.

In the end, defending S7 is a battle against time—against technology built for a bygone era and organizational inertia that resists change. The challenge is immense, but the solution is clear: transform the legacy into an asset through proactive, integrated security. The Siemens stack was built to be transparent and efficient, but in a world where every command can be exploited, transparency without control is exposure. By rethinking the architecture—hardening engineering stations, tightly controlling gateways, and continuously managing and validating assets—the industry can turn a protocol that once assumed universal trust into a secure, resilient foundation for the future.

CHAPTER 15 - ANALOG ROOTS, DIGITAL RISKS: SECURING THE 4– 20 MA BACKBONE

Below is the complete, fully integrated version of the chapter titled "Analog Roots, Digital Risks: Securing the 4–20 mA Backbone." This version retains as much of the original language as possible while weaving in new discussions on HART integration, physical security aspects, redundancy and failover, Industry 4.0 implications, and additional real-world anecdotes.

Analog signaling via the 4–20 mA current loop has for decades been the backbone of industrial process measurement —a system whose simplicity and robustness allowed it to thrive in harsh environments where electromagnetic interference, extreme temperatures, and long cable runs could otherwise corrupt data. In this design, a reading of 4 mA, commonly known as the "live zero," assures operators that even a broken cable produces an unmistakable low signal, while 20 mA defines the upper bound of measurement. This analog purity has delivered consistent reliability in countless applications ranging from water treatment to chemical processing. Its enduring success has earned it a reputation for accuracy and resilience.

Yet as industrial control systems have modernized and become intertwined with digital networks, the need to integrate these analog signals into supervisory systems has become inevitable. That integration is accomplished through 4–20 gateways— devices which convert the analog current into a digital value and package the sensor data for use in SCADA, DCS, or IIoT systems. In many cases, these gateways even incorporate additional protocols such as HART, which overlays digital communication on the 4–20 mA loop to offer richer device diagnostics and configuration data. While HART introduces flexibility, it also adds complexity and potential vulnerabilities that must be managed alongside the inherent risks of digital conversion.

This conversion process, however, does not come without a cost. Although the raw 4–20 mA signal is elegant in its determinism and simplicity, once the data is digitized it acquires a new attack surface. The gateway's software, firmware, and network interfaces can expose vulnerabilities that did not exist in the standalone analog system. Often running on standard operating systems with known flaws and sometimes left in their default configuration, these gateways become critical nodes through which sensor data flows. An attacker who compromises a 4–20 gateway can manipulate the digitized readings, cause them to report false values, or even inject entirely spurious data into the control system. Thus, while the analog side remains robust, the digitized representation is only as trustworthy as the security of the gateway that converts it.

Even as operators rely on gateways to bring legacy sensor data into the modern world, they must contend with issues of physical security. The wiring and terminal connections of the 4–20 mA system are often exposed in hazardous environments. Although the current loop is inherently resistant to electrical noise, its physical components—cable junctions, connection blocks, and terminal strips—are vulnerable to tampering. In many facilities, maintenance personnel sometimes overlook regular inspection of these elements, leaving open avenues for physical intrusion that could lead to signal manipulation. Combined with the fact that gateways are now the bridge between the analog sensor and the digital network, a breach in physical security can have cascading effects—further emphasizing that both the analog infrastructure and its digital interface must be secured.

The 4–20 gateway is not simply an isolated converter; it is a critical node whose integrity determines the accuracy of the entire control system. In its ideal operation, it relays sensor measurements in near real time, along with metadata such as timestamps, sensor identification, and calibration details. This rich detail creates an opportunity for defenders: when integrated with modern monitoring platforms like Tenable OT, Claroty, or Nozomi Networks, this telemetry forms the basis of continuous asset inventory and proactive vulnerability management. Such tools can passively capture network traffic, actively query gateways for diagnostics and firmware versions, and correlate this data with known vulnerabilities. In this way, the once-analog measurement transforms into a dynamic source of intelligence—if its digitized form is trusted.

Yet herein lies a critical weak point. When monitoring systems are deployed upstream from the gateway, they see only the gateway's reported data rather than the raw sensor outputs. This secondhand visibility forces defenders to trust that the gateway has not been compromised, misconfigured, or altered. Active scanning often fails to penetrate the gateway's translation layer, leaving a blind spot regarding the actual state of the field devices. As a result, the gateway becomes a single point of trust—and if that trust is betrayed, the entire chain of analog-to-digital conversion is at risk.

Redundancy and failover are sometimes implemented to mitigate the risk of a single gateway failure. Multiple 4–20 gateways may be installed to provide backup in the event one goes down, and such redundancy can help ensure continuous data flow. Yet redundancy also introduces complexity. Without proper coordination, different gateways might report conflicting sensor values or create opportunities for an attacker to exploit timing discrepancies. Redundant systems may also amplify the challenge of asset inventory, complicating the task of ensuring every gateway is patched, configured, and monitored consistently. Therefore, while redundancy is valuable, it must be managed carefully through strict configuration management and continuous validation of data consistency across devices.

The advent of Industry 4.0 and the increasing use of IIoT frameworks add another layer to the challenge. As digital twins, cloud-based analytics, and remote monitoring become commonplace, 4–20 gateways are not only tasked with data conversion but are integrated into vast, interconnected systems. In such architectures, sensor data is transmitted from the field all the way to cloud dashboards. Here, any weakness in the gateway's security can affect not only local control operations but also enterprise-wide decision-making. Integrated threat intelligence must extend to the analog-to-digital interface, ensuring that the valuable legacy data is not lost amid the noise of modern cyber threats.

Real-world examples abound that illustrate both the hazards and best practices of securing 4–20 gateways. In one instance, an industrial facility deploying Tenable OT in concert with Claroty and Nozomi Networks established a continuous real-time inventory of its 4–20 gateway devices. Anomalies in sensor readings at one gateway—a discrepancy between raw analog inputs and the digitized data—triggered an immediate alert. Investigation revealed that the gateway had been misconfigured, inadvertently blending signals from a decommissioned sensor with those of an active one. Because the facility had implemented proactive vulnerability management and continuous asset monitoring, the discrepancy was promptly remediated, averting a potential process upset. In another case, an automotive plant overhauled its legacy asset management practices by integrating automated scans that continuously updated its entire Siemens sensor network inventory. This approach uncovered multiple instances of unpatched firmware and misconfigured gateways, building a compelling case for gradual modernization and justifying significant investments in digital hardening even for analog infrastructures.

Ultimately, the story of 4–20 mA and its digital transformation encapsulates the broader challenges faced in industrial cybersecurity. The analog system—timeless and robust—continues to provide reliable measurement, but when its signal is digitized by a gateway, a new array of vulnerabilities emerges. The risk is not inherent in the analog technology itself, but in the interface between analog and digital, where modern cyber threats loom large. The goal is not to abandon a trusted method of measurement but to secure every link in the chain—from the sensor and its wiring to the gateway that converts its signal, and finally to the digital network that uses that data for critical decision-making.

Ensuring that 4–20 mA systems remain a trusted foundation in a digital world will require an integrated strategy: hardening gateways through rigorous patch management, securing remote management interfaces, and physically protecting wiring and connections; implementing continuous asset inventory and proactive vulnerability management to detect anomalies in real time; and embracing a cultural shift that acknowledges the risks posed by legacy systems while investing in their ongoing improvement. Industry certifications and regulatory frameworks, such as those outlined in IEC 62443, provide valuable guidelines, but true security comes from a persistent commitment to bridging the gap between proven analog reliability and the demands of modern digital control. Analog roots may be enduring, but in the modern era, the digital conversion must be as secure as the measurement itself. Only then can the robust legacy of 4–20 mA endure amid an ever-evolving cyber threat landscape.

CHAPTER 16 - DEVICE FIRMWARE: THE SILENT ATTACK SURFACE

For all the attention paid to networks, protocols, and perimeters, the truth is that the real foundation of most industrial systems lies buried much deeper—etched into flash memory, sealed behind conformal coating, and deployed onto circuit boards never meant to be revisited. Device firmware is the operating soul of the field, animating remote terminal units, programmable logic controllers, sensor gateways, and actuators. It is where logic lives and decisions are made. And yet, for all its importance, it remains one of the most neglected and vulnerable layers in operational technology.

The history of firmware in industrial systems is a study in minimalism. Early control hardware was built for reliability and cost-efficiency, not extensibility or security. Code was written to fit within a few dozen kilobytes. Memory was precious. CPUs were slow. Power consumption was constrained. Real-time performance was paramount, and every cycle had to be justified. These constraints forced developers to write lean, deterministic code—often in C or assembly, and often without the benefit of modern development tools, libraries, or security practices. The result was firmware that worked well in isolation but broke down when exposed to the unpredictability of modern networks and adversarial input.

One of the most persistent issues in industrial firmware is the lack of proper input validation. In too many cases, devices assume that received messages are well-formed, within bounds, and sent with benign intent. Parsing routines are fragile, buffer sizes are hardcoded, and bounds checking is minimal or nonexistent. Attackers have long known that malformed protocol messages—especially over serial or TCP/IP interfaces—can trigger stack overflows, heap corruption, or instruction pointer redirection. Exploiting these vulnerabilities in the field is more difficult than in typical IT systems, but not because the software is more secure. It's because the ecosystem is harder to observe and manipulate. But when the effort is made, the consequences are immediate.

In one test of a legacy fieldbus controller used in water treatment plants, a malformed Modbus write message sent over TCP caused the device to freeze completely. The issue was traced to a buffer overflow in the message parsing routine—an error that would be trivial to prevent in modern code, but which persisted in production for over a decade. The firmware version affected was still in wide use. The manufacturer had issued an advisory four years earlier, but most operators had never seen it, let alone applied it. The update process required downtime and a serial cable connection—not a click in a console, but a physical visit. For a system running 24/7, that meant no patch. No patch meant persistent risk.

Hardcoded credentials are another legacy sin that refuses to die. Many devices shipped with default passwords—sometimes visible in documentation, sometimes embedded directly in firmware strings. Others included backdoor accounts used for vendor diagnostics or manufacturing test routines. These accounts are rarely disclosed to customers, and even when found, cannot be disabled without recompiling the firmware. Tools like binwalk and firmware extraction frameworks have made it trivial for researchers—and adversaries—to locate and reverse engineer these artifacts. Once discovered, they become permanent keys. And because many devices run lightweight operating systems or custom bootloaders with no access control, gaining shell access often means full control.

One real-world case involved a power distribution automation device that ran a proprietary RTOS and included an undocumented Telnet server accessible on a hidden port. The service wasn't listed in documentation. It didn't show up in the UI. But it responded when probed directly—and accepted a six-character root password hardcoded into a diagnostic binary. That password was discovered during a firmware tear-down by an independent researcher, who disclosed it to the manufacturer. The response was muted. The vendor quietly removed the password in a later release—but never issued a bulletin or notified customers. The vulnerable version remained in service across thousands of substations. No alarms were triggered. No headlines were written. The door simply stayed open.

Much of the firmware used in industrial equipment today is not written in-house, but assembled. Vendors license real-time operating systems, embed third-party protocol stacks, and integrate generic libraries—often with little visibility into their origin or security posture. TCP/IP stacks like uIP, lwIP, or proprietary variants have been reused for decades, frequently with custom modifications that complicate patching. Even open-source components, such as embedded web servers or cryptographic libraries, are often several versions behind and compiled without basic hardening. The result is firmware built like a quilt—stitched together from dependencies that no one owns entirely, and that few can properly maintain. When a vulnerability is discovered in one of these components, it's rarely clear who's responsible for fixing it—or how long the flaw has existed.

Even when firmware updates are issued, the update mechanisms themselves are often vulnerable. Many embedded devices accept unsigned binaries, relying solely on filename conventions or delivery method for trust. Others fetch updates over unsecured channels—FTP, HTTP, or serial—from unauthenticated sources. In some cases, the device doesn't verify the firmware at all, blindly flashing whatever it receives. This opens the door to supply chain attacks, rogue technician implants, or targeted updates injected over compromised internal links. A USB port in a cabinet becomes an ingress point. A spoofed FTP server becomes a firmware delivery mechanism. In environments where updates are rare, trust in the process is often high—and that trust is easily exploited.

Over time, many organizations accumulate what amounts to shadow firmware—devices in production that no one knows how to update, support, or verify. They may be vendor-locked, their tools long deprecated. They may be protected by contracts that discourage modification. Or they may simply be too critical to touch. These devices persist in place for years, functionally invisible to modern security tools. They become ghosts in the environment—powered, trusted, and vulnerable.

Change may be coming. Regulators, security researchers, and industrial customers are increasingly demanding transparency into firmware through Software Bills of Materials. An SBOM provides a manifest of components used in a firmware image —offering visibility into inherited risk, licensing, and update status. In theory, this could transform firmware from a black box into an inspectable, governable asset. In practice, resistance is strong. Vendors worry about IP exposure, liability, and the effort of tracking decades-old components. But the pressure is mounting. In critical infrastructure, firmware is too important to remain opaque. The fight over SBOMs is just beginning—but the need is already clear.

Firmware is more than an attack surface—it's a hiding place. When an attacker implants malicious code into device firmware, that payload persists across power cycles, software updates, and even operating system reinstallation. It resides below the visibility of most endpoint detection tools and survives efforts to "clean" a compromised system. In advanced threat campaigns, attackers have used modified firmware as a platform for lateral movement, device impersonation, and long-term persistence. Once embedded, the implant becomes part of the infrastructure itself—a parasite no one can see and few tools can dislodge.

Firmware insecurity isn't just about code quality—it's also about operational culture. In the field, technicians are under pressure to keep systems running. Tools are shared between teams. USB drives move from device to device. Firmware is cloned, restored from backups, or passed along by email. In some cases, vendor tools bypass all authentication to speed up commissioning. These shortcuts are born from necessity, not negligence—but they create channels through which malware or malformed binaries can travel silently, hopping from one controller to the next under the guise of maintenance.

As awareness of firmware threats has grown, some vendors have adopted digital signatures for firmware updates. But the mere presence of a signature isn't enough. In many cases, signature verification is optional—or silently skipped when the device is in bootloader mode. Worse, some vendors use the same signing key across product lines, or fail to revoke compromised keys. Without strict enforcement and proper key management, digital signatures become security theater—a checkbox on a datasheet rather than a meaningful defense.

One of the few defenses against firmware tampering is secure boot—a cryptographic mechanism that ensures only signed firmware images can run. In modern IT hardware, secure boot is increasingly standard. In OT, it's still the exception. Many embedded systems lack hardware support for trusted execution. Others have secure boot disabled by default to support legacy code or field-level reprogramming. In theory, secure boot prevents unauthorized implants. In practice, it is often disabled for convenience—or never implemented at all.

In some hardware, the most powerful firmware isn't in the main CPU—it's in the controller beside it. Baseboard management controllers, serial maintenance ports, and out-of-band access modules often run separate firmware stacks with minimal authentication and deep control over system behavior. These auxiliary systems are rarely monitored, rarely patched, and often forgotten. But they can reboot systems, overwrite memory, or inject commands silently. For an attacker, they are a backdoor with administrative privileges built into the motherboard itself.

Firmware often carries baggage. Legacy functions, diagnostic routines, and obsolete communication methods are left in the codebase—not because they're needed, but because removing them might break something. These hidden features become backdoors no one remembers, exploitable functions that survive long past their operational relevance. Dead code doesn't stay dead—it just becomes invisible until someone figures out how to wake it up.

Some industrial devices rely not just on traditional firmware, but on programmable logic layers—field-programmable gate arrays or embedded system-on-chip configurations. These bitstreams define hardware behavior and are typically updated less frequently, if at all. But they are just as vulnerable to tampering, reverse engineering, and supply chain risk. Worse, they rarely include any cryptographic validation or access control, and modifications to the logic layer can be almost impossible to detect in the field. Like firmware, these configurations are assumed to be immutable—but they are not. Once an adversary understands the bitstream structure or the toolchain used to deploy it, manipulation becomes not only possible but persistent. Since programmable logic often governs timing-critical or safety-relevant behavior, even a subtle change can have outsized consequences—flipping relay logic, altering feedback loops, or introducing latent failure states invisible during normal operation.

Another overlooked issue is firmware reuse across product lines, industries, and application spaces. Vendors don't rewrite firmware from scratch. They reuse it across generations, across verticals, and across regional markets. A vulnerability discovered in a smart lighting controller might be just as applicable to a wastewater treatment system, an elevator control module, or a gas metering unit—because all of them run the same or similar firmware stacks, compiled from a common codebase. This portability means that the value of a single exploit is magnified. What appears to be an isolated issue can rapidly scale into a multi-sector threat, especially when organizations rely on identical devices across facilities, vendors maintain quiet update channels, and asset owners lack the visibility to map version lineage across their own infrastructure.

This quiet persistence of firmware vulnerabilities is rooted in both technical and institutional inertia. On the technical side, industrial firmware often runs on deeply embedded systems that lack standard security interfaces. Memory protections like ASLR, stack canaries, or non-executable memory regions are rare or unsupported. Logging is minimal, if present at all. Cryptographic functions may be missing or flawed due to limited CPU capabilities or poor implementation. And because many systems boot from EEPROM or flash without a secure boot process, tampering goes undetected. Attackers with physical access can extract and reflash firmware with relative ease, bypassing superficial protections and reintroducing older vulnerabilities long after they were supposedly resolved.

On the institutional side, the barriers to firmware updates are often prohibitive. Certification processes—whether driven by regulatory requirements, customer contracts, or internal QA policies—can make any code change a months-long ordeal. In nuclear, aviation, or regulated energy environments, every firmware revision may require re-qualification, testing under load, and review by third parties. This delays even critical patches and disincentivizes proactive improvement. Vendors, aware of the cost and risk associated with updates, often avoid them unless legally required or publicly shamed. And asset owners, lacking clear inventory and update tracking tools, may not even know which version of firmware is running on which device—or whether an update exists at all.

These barriers compound when third-party integration is involved. Many industrial devices include protocol converters, embedded web servers, or OEM firmware stacks licensed from smaller vendors. When a vulnerability is found in one of these components, the remediation path is unclear. Who owns the patch? Who certifies the update? Who notifies customers? The fragmentation of responsibility creates fertile ground for confusion, delay, and finger-pointing. Meanwhile, the vulnerable code remains operational, invisible to most security scans and untouched by conventional vulnerability management tools.

The scale of the issue is enormous. Large facilities may operate thousands of embedded devices, each running its own proprietary firmware stack, written years apart by different teams. These devices are not always addressable over the network. Some communicate only via serial. Others require custom software or field engineering tools to access diagnostics. In many cases, there is no automated way to extract firmware versions or validate signatures. Asset inventories list model numbers and roles—not firmware integrity or exposure. Without physical access and specialized knowledge, verifying the security state of a fleet of embedded field devices is nearly impossible.

This silent exposure has not gone unnoticed by threat actors. Nation-state groups and advanced persistent threats have demonstrated the capability to reverse engineer industrial firmware, identify custom vulnerabilities, and deploy implants designed to persist across reboots. The TRITON/Trisis malware that targeted a safety instrumented system in the Middle East was a wake-up call not only because of its intent to disrupt safety systems, but because it leveraged firmware-level understanding of the controller. That wasn't an accident. It was the product of methodical research, hardware acquisition, and detailed reverse engineering. It showed what was possible when an attacker had the time, motive, and expertise to dig below the application layer.

For less sophisticated actors, the bar is still high—but falling. Open-source firmware analysis tools, emulation environments like QEMU, and prebuilt test harnesses make it easier than ever to inspect device firmware without needing the physical hardware. Public repositories now host thousands of extracted firmware images—many pulled from manufacturer updates, downloads, or memory dumps. Once rare and esoteric, firmware analysis is becoming mainstream. And as it does, the hidden flaws of embedded systems are being exposed at a rate the industry is not prepared to handle.

The question is not whether firmware is vulnerable. It is. The question is how we account for it—how we incorporate firmware into our threat models, our asset inventories, and our patching strategies. That requires a cultural shift as much as a technical one. Security teams must be empowered to look below the surface. Procurement policies must demand access to update channels, vulnerability disclosures, and cryptographic authenticity for firmware releases. Operators must push vendors to eliminate hardcoded secrets, implement secure boot, and build firmware stacks with modern memory protections. And the industry must acknowledge that the devices we trust the most—the ones closest to the physical world—are often the ones we've verified the least.

There is no one solution. Firmware security is a long-tail problem, full of nuance, legacy, and embedded risk. But ignoring it won't make it go away. The attackers have already noticed. It's time the defenders did too. Because beneath every protocol, every packet, and every process control loop, there's a silent attack surface, humming along faithfully. Until the moment it doesn't.

PART III
Architectural Realities and Points of Entry

CHAPTER 17 -
FLATTENED NETWORKS
AND FRAGILE
SEGMENTATION

Industrial network diagrams are often works of fiction. They portray elegant layers of isolation, with clean zones, clear boundaries, and only the most deliberate connections threading between them. The perimeter is defined, the DMZ is air-gapped, and the control network is locked down—at least on paper. But in practice, these diagrams rarely match reality. The architectures deployed in the field are often flat, improvised, and decades old. Segmentation exists as a concept but not as a constraint. Devices talk freely across VLANs. Firewalls are permissive or missing. And the assumed protections between layers are more cultural than technical.

The flatness of industrial networks is not accidental. It is the legacy of growth without redesign, of adding new systems to old ones without rethinking how they interact. A facility that began with a single PLC rack might now have multiple buildings, thousands of devices, and dozens of vendors—all layered onto a topology that was never intended to scale. Each expansion brought with it new switches, new cables, and new IP ranges—but not necessarily new security models. Devices were dropped into the same subnet because it worked, because it was fast, and because no one had the time or political capital to refactor the architecture. Over time, segmentation eroded, not because it was opposed, but because it was inconvenient.

VLANs were meant to be the answer—virtual segmentation that could separate traffic at Layer 2 without physical rewiring. But VLANs are only as good as the configurations that support them, and in practice, those configurations are often flawed. Industrial switches are frequently unmanaged or mismanaged. Tagging is inconsistent. Trunk ports are overprovisioned. In some cases, all VLANs are permitted on all ports by default, rendering the segmentation meaningless. Broadcast traffic crosses boundaries. Devices auto-discover across supposed isolation zones. And VLAN hopping attacks—long a concern in IT—are not even considered in most OT threat models.

In flat industrial networks, where trust is implicit and Layer 2 visibility is limited, an attacker with even modest access can launch attacks that go unnoticed. ARP spoofing, DHCP poisoning, and MAC flooding are trivially effective in environments where protections like dynamic ARP inspection or port security are absent. A malicious device can impersonate a default gateway, intercept Modbus TCP traffic, or hijack communications between HMIs and controllers—all without generating alerts. These attacks don't require zero-days or privilege escalation. They require proximity, persistence, and a flat topology.

One of the most common segmentation failures comes not from the switches, but from the workstations. Engineering laptops often have dual NICs, or a wired connection to the control network alongside corporate Wi-Fi. These machines become unintentional bridges—linking zones that were never meant to talk. In some cases, the laptop runs vendor tools, email clients, VPN clients, and HMI software simultaneously. The segmentation fails not because of malice, but because no one considered what would happen when the same device touched both worlds.

Worse, segmentation failures are often silent. There are no alarms when a vendor system suddenly gains access to the plant floor network. There are no red flags when a camera management server can ping a PLC. These connections are technically possible, and so they happen. The firewall rules allow them, or the VLANs are bridged in a forgotten switch, or someone needed access for testing and never removed it. This quiet collapse of segmentation is how attackers move laterally—not with exploits, but with reach.

The myth of the air gap still lingers in many facilities. Engineers will insist that their critical networks are isolated, even as those networks send alerts to a cloud dashboard or receive firmware updates via a technician's laptop. The air gap is not a physical reality. It is a belief system—a collective illusion that isolation can be inferred from intent. In one real-world incident, a plant operator claimed with confidence that the control system was air-gapped. In practice, the HMI was connected via a USB-over-IP bridge to a corporate terminal used for remote support. That bridge was active 24/7, routed over a shared switch, and invisible to the plant's network diagrams. The gap wasn't just bridged—it had never existed.

In many architectures, segmentation is justified by the idea that certain systems only receive data. A historian, a dashboard, a monitoring node—these are assumed to be passive. But protocols like OPC Classic don't distinguish clearly between clients and servers. A "read-only" system can be coerced into initiating outbound connections, performing writes, or executing remote calls, simply because of how the underlying protocol handles binding. What was meant to be a one-way pipe becomes a two-way street, and no one notices—because the system still displays data, even as it listens to commands it should never hear.

Segmentation can't protect what it doesn't see. In more than one facility, segmentation was confidently deployed—between the enterprise and control networks, between zones and cells. But buried inside a cabinet was a small 4G modem installed by a vendor during commissioning. It provided "emergency access" via a web portal in another country. No one documented it. No one monitored it. And no firewall rule could control it—because it wasn't on the network. It was beside it. That kind of bypass renders even the best segmentation meaningless.

Vendor access is the sharp edge of this problem. Remote vendors need to troubleshoot, patch, and configure equipment that operators don't fully understand and can't modify. To enable this, VPN tunnels are deployed—sometimes through firewalls, sometimes through cellular modems, sometimes through unmanaged remote desktop gateways. These tunnels are often permanent, bidirectional, and poorly monitored. Once connected, vendors can access far more than their slice of the environment. In one case, a vendor VPN intended to reach a turbine controller also allowed access to the plant's safety system and the historian database—because all three were on the same subnet. No one had reviewed the route table. No one had restricted access. The tunnel was convenient, so it stayed.

Modern industrial protocols are built to bridge—across sites, through firewalls, and between clouds and controllers. OPC UA and MQTT allow multiplexed sessions, publish-subscribe models, and remote configuration via the same port that carries telemetry. The problem isn't the protocol—it's the assumption that a single port implies a single purpose. Segmentation rules permit port 8883 for MQTT telemetry, but embedded in that session is a subscription change, or worse, a remote firmware update. The protocol becomes a Trojan horse—segmentation thinks it's seeing data, but what it's allowing is control.

Segmentation on paper does not equal segmentation in enforcement. Many plants maintain detailed architecture diagrams that show clear divisions: Level 0 sensors, Level 1 PLCs, Level 2 HMIs, and Level 3 corporate interfaces. But in reality, devices from Level 2 and Level 1 share VLANs. Firewalls permit "any any" for vendor ports. Windows laptops are dual-homed with one interface on the control network and another on the business LAN. These aren't oversights—they're accommodations. They exist because someone needed to get something working, and security was not part of the conversation.

Even where segmentation is technically implemented, enforcement is fragile. Industrial firewalls may lack the protocol awareness to make meaningful decisions. Rules are written once and never audited. An engineer might open ports to debug a commissioning issue and forget to close them. Or worse, a vendor may request persistent access "just in case." Over time, the rule sets become bloated, permissive, and opaque. When something goes wrong, the default response is to open access further—just to see if that fixes the issue.

Misconfigured segmentation also causes unintentional outages. When VLANs are improperly pruned, devices can't discover each other. When broadcast domains span too wide, devices collide. When routing is misaligned, packets take unexpected paths —sometimes through slower or overloaded switches, causing latency or jitter in time-sensitive control loops. These aren't security failures in the traditional sense. They're operational instabilities caused by weak architecture. And because they impact production, they're resolved by bypassing segmentation, not enforcing it.

This collapse is often discovered too late—during incident response, during red team exercises, or during a failed compliance audit. Teams discover that supposedly isolated segments are reachable via maintenance ports. That wireless access points bridge VLANs. That old switches route untagged traffic between "isolated" networks. In one audit, a supposedly segmented engineering workstation was reachable from the corporate office via a forgotten static route configured years earlier to troubleshoot a batch problem. That route was never removed. No one remembered it existed. But it was there—and it worked.

While segmentation often fails in software, there is one class of architectural control that enforces it with physical certainty: the data diode. Unlike a firewall, a diode doesn't rely on rule sets or port filters. It enforces one-way communication using hardware —typically a fiber link or optical gate that strips the return path entirely. When properly deployed, a diode guarantees that data can flow from one network zone to another—but never back. No amount of misconfiguration, no protocol abuse, no vendor tunnel can change that. It is segmentation by subtraction.

Diodes are often deployed between control networks and higher-level IT systems—most commonly in environments like nuclear, defense, or regulated energy where assurance is required. In these networks, the historian may receive data from the plant floor via a diode, but no write or command traffic can ever return. It's a simple model, and that simplicity is its strength. Where VLANs fail silently and firewalls grow porous, diodes remain immutable. Yet they are underused—viewed as exotic, expensive, or too rigid for daily operations. In reality, they are one of the few mechanisms that reliably enforce trust boundaries, even in the face of human error and software fragility.

The human element compounds the fragility. Segmentation plans often fail because they are not understood by the people who operate the systems. Operators know the process, not the topology. Vendors know their product, not the network. And security teams, often brought in after deployment, have no context for why certain ports were opened or why certain paths exist. The segmentation is fragile because the knowledge required to maintain it is fragmented—and over time, that knowledge decays.

To fix this decay, organizations must acknowledge that segmentation is not a one-time configuration. It is a living control that requires visibility, enforcement, and governance. It must be tested, monitored, and reviewed. Devices must be mapped not just by IP but by function. Firewalls must be rule-based, not permit-all. VLANs must be pruned, tagged, and validated. And above all, the architecture must reflect the reality of how the network is used—not just how it was intended to work when the diagram was drawn.

Segmentation done right is powerful. It limits blast radius. It slows lateral movement. It enforces trust boundaries. But segmentation done wrong—assumed, misconfigured, or ignored—is worse than none at all. It creates a false sense of security that allows risk to flourish in silence. The architecture doesn't fail loudly. It fails quietly, invisibly, until someone finds a path they shouldn't be able to take—and no one notices until they already have.

CHAPTER 18 - IMPLEMENTING MONITORING, DETECTION, AND RESPONSE IN OT ENVIRONMENTS

For decades, industrial control systems were assumed to operate in a vacuum—physically isolated, deterministic, and so reliable that deviations from normal behavior were more often chalked up to mechanical issues than malicious intent. But digital convergence changed that illusion. The same integration that enabled remote diagnostics, centralized visibility, and automation also invited risk. OT networks, once analog fortresses, became susceptible to many of the same intrusions long endemic to IT networks. But while the nature of the threat might be familiar, the context is not. Defending OT systems requires methods shaped by uptime imperatives, legacy limitations, and the absolute priority of safety.

At the heart of any detection capability lies visibility. Without the ability to observe network traffic, device behavior, and control system events, anomaly detection becomes guesswork. In IT environments, logging and telemetry are mature disciplines. Servers stream detailed logs, and endpoint detection tools provide real-time insight into process behavior. But most legacy OT devices were never designed to generate logs, much less security-relevant ones. Their job was simple: process inputs, execute instructions, and maintain operations. Memory, CPU cycles, protocols, and communications interfaces were tightly constrained. Asking these devices to participate in modern telemetry is like asking a rotary phone to send a video message.

The gap between what OT systems can provide and what modern security tools expect has forced defenders to get creative. Passive monitoring has become the default strategy. Rather than querying devices directly—which could introduce risk or interfere with sensitive operations—engineers deploy span ports and network taps. These silent observers collect mirrored traffic from switches or hubs, capturing communication patterns between PLCs, HMIs, controllers, sensors, and engineering workstations. Done correctly, this respects the foundational principle of OT cybersecurity: do no harm.

However, passive techniques can only go so far. They offer visibility into network behavior but rarely expose the inner state of devices themselves. That's where native protocol queries enter the picture. Tools like Nozomi Networks, Claroty, Dragos, Radiflow, and Tenable OT are designed to communicate using the same languages—Modbus, DNP3, EtherNet/IP, PROFINET— that OT devices already understand. Instead of probing for generic metadata, these platforms ask precise questions tailored to each device type, extracting configuration details, firmware versions, logic changes, and status indicators.

Tenable OT, for example, blends passive monitoring with protocol-aware querying to capture a unified picture of configuration states and unauthorized changes. It integrates with Tenable's broader vulnerability management suite, bridging IT/OT domains in a way that makes sense to both security analysts and control engineers. Nozomi Networks' Guardian platform provides topology mapping, firmware inspection, and behavioral baselining, using both passive techniques and active polling where appropriate. Claroty's Continuous Threat Detection system focuses on deep packet inspection and protocol-specific analysis, offering insight into asset behavior and known vulnerabilities. Dragos distinguishes itself through intelligence-driven detection, leveraging incident-derived behavioral signatures and response playbooks crafted for ICS contexts. Radiflow's iSID platform, meanwhile, supports both passive and active monitoring, excelling in network segmentation analysis and policy enforcement.

What all of these tools share is the ability to extend visibility far beyond what legacy OT systems were ever built to support. But implementation must proceed cautiously. Legacy devices, by design, prioritize predictability over flexibility. Even well-formed queries can destabilize them if handled poorly. That's why all active monitoring should begin in a testbed—ideally using a digital twin or parallel infrastructure that mimics production behavior without putting live operations at risk. Testing should validate not just data accuracy but the impact of polling intervals, query formats, and exception handling under load. Once deployed, active tools must be carefully tuned to avoid overwhelming fragile endpoints or introducing latency into time-sensitive control loops. In OT environments, the price of overreach is measured not in packet loss but in production downtime—or worse.

Beyond safety, there are strategic considerations. These tools are expensive—not only to license but to deploy, integrate, and maintain. Their effectiveness depends less on default configurations and more on the people behind them. A well-tuned detection engine, supported by analysts who understand the protocols and operations it observes, can illuminate threats with surgical precision. But an untuned system becomes a liability, raising irrelevant alerts, missing important signals, or undermining the trust of engineers. Skilled deployment teams don't just install the platform—they translate between operational nuances and cyber indicators, calibrate thresholds that reflect process variability, and avoid triggering fatigue through excessive false positives.

Data volume adds another challenge. These platforms collect everything—device metadata, command sequences, protocol chatter, error conditions. The result is an avalanche of information, most of which is noise until filtered and contextualized. Analysts must determine which events matter, which conditions warrant escalation, and which anomalies are merely symptoms of normal variation. This tuning isn't a "set it and forget it" task. It's a living process, refined as systems evolve, as vendors issue updates, and as the facility's operational rhythms shift with maintenance cycles or process changes.

Detection itself hinges on understanding normal. In IT, baselining is straightforward—users log in, access applications, and transmit data in relatively predictable ways. OT environments are messier. A plant might house decades of equipment, each with its own behavior patterns, legacy quirks, and undocumented workarounds. Communication rhythms aren't always regular, and bursts of traffic may align with human activity rather than machine logic. Security personnel must work hand-in-hand with engineers to interpret what's expected, what's unusual, and what signals true risk. A spike in DNP3 traffic might be a scan—or just a recalibration event. An unexpected controller message could be malware—or routine diagnostics.

Signature-based detection, the IT default, is poorly suited for this terrain. Too few known malware samples target OT systems, and even when they do, their behavior blends into complex industrial noise. Behavioral analytics and machine learning offer a better path—if deployed with caution. By analyzing long-term communication trends, these models can highlight deviations without knowing exactly what to look for. Still, context remains essential. A PLC reaching out to an engineering workstation it's never touched before may not be infected—but it deserves a closer look.

This balance—between sensitivity and specificity—is delicate. In environments where uptime and safety are paramount, even a false alarm can have serious consequences. Fatigue is dangerous. If alerts become too frequent or too vague, operators will ignore them. Trust erodes quickly. That's why tuning must be a shared exercise, not the responsibility of security alone. OT engineers, operations staff, and cybersecurity teams must jointly define what constitutes suspicious behavior, which alerts matter most, and how to respond. Playbooks should be tailored not just to threat types but to process consequences. A failed logon in an IT system is a minor issue. In an OT environment, it could mean unauthorized logic access—or an engineer using the wrong credentials.

Modern monitoring platforms bring real-time analytics and anomaly detection, but without careful tuning, they risk overwhelming operators with false positives. Alert fatigue is a real threat in these environments. If personnel are constantly bombarded with non-actionable notifications, true signals may be missed. Effective monitoring isn't just about data—it's about context, and the ability to filter noise from insight.

Incident response in OT is its own discipline. The tactics used in IT—quarantining systems, rebooting endpoints, pushing patches—can be catastrophic in a control environment. An improperly timed shutdown might halt production, damage equipment, or trigger emergency safety systems. That's why every action in OT must be mapped out in advance. Response playbooks must reflect the technical and procedural constraints of physical processes. Escalation paths must be rehearsed and understood. Who approves containment? Can a firewall rule be applied in real time? Should systems be switched to manual control? None of these decisions should be made ad hoc.

Tabletop exercises, conducted with OT and IT personnel side by side, reveal the friction points. They surface misunderstandings, highlight decision-making gaps, and build trust across disciplines. These sessions are not check-the-box compliance efforts—they are survival training. They simulate not only how malware propagates, but how the plant should react. What happens if the HMI is compromised? If a remote vendor's credentials are used to push rogue logic? These scenarios must be confronted before the real thing occurs.

Some organizations are beginning to reflect this maturity in their SOCs. Fusion centers now correlate IT and OT telemetry, drawing connections between email-based phishing and credential misuse in engineering networks. But visibility is only half the equation. Analysts need fluency. Most are trained in IT concepts—ports, protocols, threats—but few understand ladder logic, scan rates, or safety interlocks. Bridging this gap may require dedicated OT analysts, embedded in the SOC, or a parallel OT security function that interfaces with the broader cybersecurity team. The structure matters less than the outcome: a continuous dialogue between those who defend networks and those who operate processes.

Tools themselves are evolving to support this. Platforms now offer dashboards that speak the language of both engineering and cybersecurity. They provide real-time maps of device interactions, logic summaries, and alerts based on process-aware thresholds. Deployment strategies often incorporate data diodes or unidirectional gateways to ensure that visibility flows out but never in—preserving the integrity of control systems while enabling detection capabilities. Integration with SIEMs, threat intel feeds, and machine learning engines allows these tools to position OT anomalies within a broader attack narrative.

Yet no tool can compensate for poor governance. Monitoring must be woven into policy. Who reviews alerts? How fast? What constitutes an incident? How are third-party contractors monitored? Answers to these questions must be documented, updated, and enforced. A well-instrumented environment with no clear escalation policy is like a state-of-the-art smoke detector in an empty building.

Ultimately, monitoring, detection, and response in OT

environments is about reconciling opposing forces—visibility versus risk, vigilance versus disruption, automation versus human insight. It is about looking deeply into systems never meant to be seen and translating what they reveal into action without breaking what they sustain. It is a process of building trust across disciplines, between engineers and analysts, vendors and operators. And it is a journey toward resilience—not just for the networks and devices under watch, but for the organizations that depend on them.

The threats will keep coming. Adversaries will adapt. Legacy vulnerabilities will persist. But with persistent visibility, refined detection, and disciplined response—coordinated across silos and grounded in operational reality—these systems can be defended. And when the silence of a humming control room is broken by something unfamiliar, the right systems will be listening, ready to turn that whisper into a warning.

CHAPTER 19 - SUPPLY CHAIN PROTOCOL POLLUTION

Most organizations trust the protocol stacks running in their industrial systems without ever having seen them. A controller supports Modbus, so it must follow the Modbus specification. A gateway translates DNP3, so it must behave like any other. An HMI vendor promises OPC compliance, so the software should be interoperable and safe. But that assumption—that protocol behavior equals protocol integrity—is often wrong. Because many of the stacks in use today weren't written by the vendors who sell them. They were licensed, inherited, bought, copied, or patched over time, becoming hybrids of specification and convenience. And when protocols are delivered through a supply chain, they carry not only functionality but risk —silently polluting the environment with hidden behaviors, undocumented quirks, and vulnerabilities that no one truly owns.

Protocol pollution begins with reuse. Few vendors write their own protocol stacks from scratch. It takes time, domain knowledge, and meticulous testing to implement a reliable stack for industrial use. Instead, vendors purchase implementations from third parties, often small firms that specialize in embedded communications. Others use open-source libraries, written years ago and updated sporadically. Some vendors buy firmware packages that bundle multiple protocols—Modbus, DNP3, IEC 60870-5, BACnet—into a single image compiled with generic configuration options. These stacks are portable, lightweight, and easy to deploy across devices. But they are rarely inspected, fuzzed, or reviewed with the rigor those protocols deserve.

In many cases, protocol stacks aren't even written by the vendors that ship them. They originate from contract developers or offshore ODMs, often operating in regulatory environments with very different norms. Some of the most widely deployed protocol logic originates from development houses in regions where security assurance is secondary to functionality and cost. The issue isn't one of nationality, but of transparency. If you don't know who wrote the stack, who audited it, or where it was compiled, then every protocol function is a leap of faith. You're not just trusting the vendor— you're trusting their entire upstream chain.

Over time, these shared stacks accumulate entropy. One vendor may tweak a timeout parameter. Another may bypass input validation for performance. A third may add a proprietary function code, undocumented and non-standard, to support internal diagnostics. What began as a standards-based implementation slowly drifts into something else—something that still speaks the protocol but does so with differences invisible until they matter. These differences rarely show up in integration testing, which focuses on success paths. They emerge only when devices miscommunicate, fail open, or crash under malformed input. At that point, the problem isn't just in the stack—it's in every device that shares that stack across the entire environment.

Many of these stacks are not standalone binaries. They are compiled directly into the firmware itself. That means even if a protocol is disabled in configuration—say, turned off in a drop-down menu or unchecked in a web interface—the parsing logic often remains in memory. It still accepts traffic. It still allocates buffers. It still processes malformed requests. The stack is present, dormant but active, because removing it entirely would require recompilation and retesting of the entire firmware package. This creates a kind of phantom exposure: the service is invisible to administrators, but fully visible to an attacker who knows where to look.

Legacy integrations make this worse. Many industrial environments are layered with generations of equipment, from new smart relays to controllers that predate modern cybersecurity. To ensure backward compatibility, vendors keep legacy protocol support in place—often untouched for decades. The Modbus implementation in a 1999 RTU may still be running in newer devices via binary duplication. These copies are rarely updated. They persist not because they are secure, but because they are understood, or at least believed to be. The older the integration, the more likely it is to include hardcoded function codes, non-standard framing, or workarounds for issues long forgotten. These ghosts of compatibility become permanent features—protocol artifacts passed from device to device like genetic mutations.

And those mutations are rarely tested. While fuzzing is common in modern software development, most industrial vendors do not apply fuzz testing to their protocol implementations. Even when tools exist, they are brittle, proprietary, or require deep customization. Asset owners, for their part, rarely run fuzzing tools against production equipment for fear of causing faults or lockups. That means protocol stacks often go untested under malformed input until an adversary—or a researcher—pushes them to the breaking point.

Certification bodies compound the problem by validating behavior, not security. Most protocol conformance testing is functional—it verifies that a stack responds correctly to expected inputs under ideal conditions. But it rarely probes malformed packets, corner cases, timing bugs, or fuzzed input. Devices pass certification not because they are resilient, but because they answer the right questions the right way. As a result, many insecure or brittle implementations carry compliance seals. They're trusted because they've been tested, but those tests rarely mimic the hostile, unpredictable conditions seen in the field.

Proprietary extensions are another vector. In theory, industrial protocol standards define clean boundaries. But in practice, vendors extend these standards to meet product-specific needs. A Modbus stack may implement custom function codes outside the public registry. A DNP3 device may include vendor-specific object groups. An OPC Classic server may expose proprietary COM interfaces undocumented in any client SDK. These extensions are often opaque to customers—and incompatible with security tools or interoperability tests. Worse, they often ignore or violate the assumptions of the protocol they modify. They behave like standards until you look closely. Then they start to diverge.

In some cases, protocol mutation is not just an accident —it's a business strategy. Vendors fork standards to create lock-in. They advertise compliance, but only within their ecosystem. Customers that buy into one product line find that other vendors' tools don't work properly—not because of true incompatibility, but because the standard was subtly modified. These deviations are often undocumented. They become another layer of opacity that interferes with interoperability, visibility, and security inspection. A scanner built for the real protocol won't recognize the altered one. A defense tool tuned for the standard can't see the fork.

One case involved a widely deployed Modbus gateway that implemented a proprietary passthrough mode. When triggered by a specific function code, the gateway forwarded traffic to a secondary serial bus with no filtering. That function code was not documented. It was used by the vendor's configuration software to push updates. But it could also be used by anyone who discovered it—including attackers. The function bypassed authentication, wrote directly to memory addresses, and allowed command injection from the Ethernet interface to any connected field device. The vendor didn't consider it a vulnerability—because it was "not part of normal operation." But it was reachable. And in a flat network, reachable means exploitable.

Some modern stacks attempt to be helpful by supporting auto-discovery or dynamic negotiation of capabilities. That convenience comes at a cost. Every negotiation introduces complexity—and every complexity expands the attack surface. An attacker can spoof discovery packets, trick a device into enabling insecure legacy modes, or trigger latent code paths that were never meant to run in production. Auto-discovery makes integration easier. It also makes protocol behavior unpredictable, especially in hybrid environments where discovery messages from one vendor may trigger unexpected behavior in another.

Trust in the supply chain extends beyond firmware and hardware—it extends to the protocol level, where flaws replicate silently across products and environments. In one incident, a utility operator discovered that two different vendor devices —an HMI panel and a power meter—crashed under the same malformed BACnet packet. The root cause was a shared open-source stack used in both products, compiled from the same source and vulnerable to the same unchecked buffer. Neither vendor had disclosed the dependency. Neither had tested the failure mode. Both devices claimed BACnet compliance. And both fell offline when tested with the same probe.

Some of the most widely used protocol relays today are cloud-connected gateways—IoT edge devices that bridge legacy serial systems with cloud services. These are often built from SDKs, Yocto images, embedded Linux distributions, and open-source protocol handlers. The box itself carries a vendor's logo, but inside it may contain a half-dozen upstream components with different maintainers and patch histories. When a vulnerability is discovered in one layer—say, the MQTT client library—there's no easy way to trace whether it affects all deployments. There is no centralized update process. There is no list of who inherited what. The supply chain becomes a mesh, and no one has a complete view.

Even within a single device, protocol pollution can be amplified by shared logic. To conserve memory, some firmware reuses parsers across different protocols. A buffer overflow in a BACnet parser might also affect how Modbus requests are handled —because they rely on the same decoding functions. The vulnerability isn't in the protocol. It's in the shared assumptions behind them. These shared routines make maintenance easier for developers, but they create nonlinear risk. One vulnerability can ripple across multiple stacks, invisible to everyone until an exploit ties the pieces together.

Sometimes the problem isn't the active code, but the remnants. Protocol stacks are rarely rewritten from scratch. Old handlers are deprecated in configuration, commented out, or removed from documentation—but they're not removed from the binary. That dead code still exists in flash memory. It may still process packets. It may still respond under specific conditions. What was meant to be inert becomes another form of ghost logic— forgotten, undocumented, and dangerous.

These shared dependencies complicate incident response. When a protocol vulnerability is disclosed, it's often unclear how many devices are affected—or which vendors used the flawed implementation. Vulnerability advisories may reference a component library or stack name unfamiliar to customers. The devices themselves may not expose version numbers or fingerprints that help with identification. And because protocol behavior is usually black-boxed—observed only during successful operation—many asset owners lack any way to test for the issue themselves. As a result, protocol vulnerabilities become supply chain problems. They require disclosure, inventory, and patching across products that were never intended to be updated in the field.

Protocol-aware firewalls are often assumed to be the answer. These tools claim to enforce behavior, validate function codes, and inspect deep payloads. But when stacks deviate from the standard—when they include proprietary extensions, malformed states, or undocumented negotiation paths—those firewalls can't keep up. They allow traffic they should reject. They fail to parse malformed messages. They quietly miss what they were meant to catch. And because they don't generate errors, no one notices the blind spot.

Software bills of materials (SBOMs) may eventually help clarify these relationships. By exposing the components, libraries, and source lineage of protocol stacks, SBOMs offer a way to track inherited risk. But most industrial vendors are not ready for that level of transparency. Many do not track component versions internally. Others fear IP exposure or customer scrutiny. Some worry that revealing too much will spark unnecessary alarm. Until that changes, protocol pollution will remain a hidden threat—present in devices that pass certification, pass testing, and pass visual inspection, but fail under real-world pressure.

Even where vendors are transparent, the problem persists because many industrial products are field-programmed with configurable protocols. A device may allow the user to enable Modbus, DNP3, or IEC 104 depending on the deployment. These options are convenient—but they also enable insecure stacks to be activated post-deployment without proper scrutiny. A technician may enable legacy DNP3 in plaintext mode for integration with a nearby RTU. No one checks whether the stack has been patched. The risk is not static. It depends on how the device is configured, and how often those configurations are reviewed.

In some cases, protocol behavior is modified not just by configuration, but by the underlying operating system or TCP/IP stack. Timing behaviors, retransmission quirks, and buffer limitations can all impact how a protocol functions in practice. Two devices running the same protocol version may behave differently under load—especially if one uses a stripped-down embedded OS and the other runs Linux or VxWorks. These differences are rarely documented or tested. They emerge in failure scenarios, creating subtle incompatibilities that can be exploited by adversaries or cause cascading faults.

The protocol itself may also be extended or embedded inside other services—tunneled over VPN, wrapped in HTTPS, or exposed via web interfaces. In one case, an energy analytics platform used a REST API to push Modbus function calls through a cloud gateway to field devices. The API required a key, but the Modbus calls it generated were unauthenticated, unlogged, and unbounded. Because the protocol was nested inside another, it bypassed inspection. This stacking of protocols—common in IIoT deployments—creates new paths of execution that fall outside traditional security models. The stack works. The data moves. The threat hides.

And that is the core challenge of protocol pollution. It is not visible in architecture diagrams. It is not obvious in traffic captures. It is not declared in procurement. It is inherited, embedded, and propagated through trust—trust in the vendor, trust in the standard, trust in the component source. That trust is often misplaced. And once broken, it is difficult to reestablish.

To fix this, organizations must ask new questions—not just what protocols are supported, but how they are implemented. Not just what devices are compliant, but which stacks they share. Protocol behavior must be profiled, not assumed. Dependencies must be disclosed, not buried. And field upgrades must be reviewed not just for functionality, but for the protocol logic they introduce. Insecure communication doesn't always come from adversaries. Sometimes, it's delivered in shrink wrap —signed, supported, and already plugged in.

CHAPTER 20 - SBOMS, TESTING, AND THE PROBLEM OF UNKNOWN BEHAVIOR

When engineers first placed software into industrial control systems, visibility into that software was nearly perfect—after all, the developers often sat just down the hall. The hardware was well-documented, the software painstakingly commented, and if something unexpected happened, you could walk directly to the developer and ask why. Over time, as industry expanded and supply chains lengthened, that intimate knowledge faded into obscurity. By the time most devices reached end-users, they were sealed black boxes, shipped with software whose origins were distant, whose internals were opaque, and whose behaviors were largely unknown.

As incidents increased in frequency and impact, security teams and regulators searched for ways to regain visibility into these increasingly hidden stacks of software. The concept of Software Bills of Materials—SBOMs—emerged as a way to list software ingredients clearly, the way food labels list nutritional information. An SBOM would tell asset owners exactly what libraries, components, and dependencies existed inside their equipment, revealing hidden vulnerabilities, licensing risks, and supply chain concerns. It was a logical, powerful idea, embraced enthusiastically across critical infrastructure sectors.

Yet, as with many logical, powerful ideas, reality proved more complicated. In industrial environments, SBOMs were often challenging to generate accurately and even harder to use effectively. Many legacy industrial controllers contained software assembled over decades, with dependencies layered deep beneath proprietary firmware. Manufacturers sometimes had no definitive record of what went into a device twenty years earlier. Some software stacks were amalgams of custom code, open-source projects, and undocumented third-party binaries, impossible to inventory completely. An SBOM can only document what's known—leaving significant blind spots precisely where risks might be greatest.

Maintaining and updating SBOMs presented additional operational challenges. Frequent software updates, patching, and vendor changes could quickly render SBOMs outdated, raising questions about who was responsible for maintaining these lists and how frequently updates should occur. Without practical integration into asset management and lifecycle processes, the utility of SBOMs diminished rapidly.

Even when SBOMs were accurate, another complication emerged: knowing what's inside a device isn't the same as knowing how that device behaves. An ingredient list doesn't tell you how the cake tastes or how it will react when placed under heat. Similarly, knowing a controller uses an open-source TCP/IP stack vulnerable to specific exploits is helpful, but it doesn't tell you if or how that vulnerability is practically exploitable in its particular implementation or environment. The SBOM revealed risks, but not necessarily outcomes. It opened the door for more questions rather than providing definitive answers.

This is why, alongside SBOMs, the practice of testing gained prominence. Fuzz testing—subjecting software and protocols to unexpected inputs to observe how they behave—became one of the most important defensive practices. Security teams, researchers, and vendors alike embraced fuzzers as ways to uncover hidden weaknesses that static analysis or code audits missed. Unlike static inspection, fuzzing treated software as a dynamic entity, observing real-world behavior under stress. It was practical, pragmatic, and insightful.

Fuzz testing, in essence, involves systematically bombarding a software interface or protocol with randomized, malformed, or deliberately erroneous inputs to observe its reaction. By doing so, security researchers can uncover vulnerabilities, bugs, and unexpected behavior that traditional testing methods often miss. Unlike structured testing, which verifies predefined behaviors, fuzz testing thrives precisely because it's unpredictable. Its value comes from its randomness—the potential to find weaknesses hidden deep within the software logic or protocol design, beyond what any human tester could anticipate.

Yet the very randomness that gives fuzz testing its power also creates significant risks, especially within operational industrial environments. Industrial control systems are typically built with precise expectations: specific packet sequences, carefully timed commands, and well-formed inputs. They often lack robust error handling for unexpected scenarios, not out of negligence, but because these systems were never intended to operate in adversarial or chaotic conditions. Thus, sending unpredictable inputs can trigger unintended—and sometimes disastrous—responses.

For example, fuzz testing an industrial controller in a live manufacturing process might reveal vulnerabilities, but it can also inadvertently halt operations by causing the controller to crash, reboot, or enter a fault state. In worst-case scenarios, malformed packets could trigger physical actions—such as valves opening or closing unexpectedly, pumps shutting down, or safety systems activating erroneously. Even in lab environments, fuzz testing can physically damage equipment or corrupt firmware, requiring expensive repairs or replacements. These scenarios are not hypothetical; they are very real, making fuzz testing both uniquely valuable and particularly dangerous in operational contexts.

Then there were protocols themselves. Legacy protocols like Modbus, DNP3, or proprietary vendor interfaces were rarely designed with formal verification or fuzz testing in mind. These protocols often assumed friendly, predictable environments, with carefully defined inputs and limited error-handling requirements. Subjecting them to rigorous fuzz testing could yield unexpected, sometimes inexplicable results —devices freezing, connections dropping, controllers rebooting at random intervals. The results were not just vulnerabilities, but bizarre and unpredictable behaviors that defied clear explanation, let alone easy remediation.

Formal verification promised a more rigorous approach: mathematically proving software correctness. In theory, formal methods could guarantee that software behaved precisely as designed, adhering strictly to defined specifications. But formal verification faced even greater barriers in legacy industrial contexts. Most legacy software wasn't written with formal verification in mind. Often, no formal specification existed, only decades of accumulated functionality and undocumented feature creep. Even attempting formal verification required reverse-engineering layers of code, reconstructing specifications from scratch—often impossible tasks when dealing with proprietary or undocumented source code.

Reverse engineering, a necessary step for understanding undocumented legacy software, introduced further complexity. It was costly, time-consuming, legally fraught, and often yielded incomplete or imprecise results. Reverse engineering often revealed partial knowledge rather than complete visibility, complicating vulnerability identification and remediation efforts.

The practical integration of security testing into lifecycle management was similarly challenging. Organizations struggled to balance rigorous testing with the operational safety required in critical environments. Security teams needed carefully controlled conditions to safely conduct testing without interrupting critical operations. Balancing these constraints required thoughtful, deliberate practices embedded within procurement and maintenance cycles.

Given these limitations, continuous behavior and communications monitoring become essential defensive strategies. Establishing clear operational baselines for normal protocol interactions enables security teams to quickly detect deviations or unexpected communications. Even without complete knowledge of a protocol's internal workings, anomalies—such as new devices appearing on the network, unexpected communication patterns, or abnormal command sequences—can provide critical early warnings. Proactive monitoring doesn't require perfect understanding; it demands vigilance and a readiness to respond swiftly when behavior diverges from established norms.

In practice, then, SBOMs, fuzz testing, reverse engineering, and formal verification each provided critical insights but failed to fully illuminate the darkness surrounding industrial protocol software. The fundamental problem remained one of unknown and unknowable behavior. Each of these techniques assumed, at some level, that software and protocols behave predictably. But industrial software—especially legacy software—rarely conforms neatly to those assumptions.

This leaves industrial security in a precarious place. SBOMs are valuable but incomplete. Fuzz testing is powerful but risky. Formal verification is rigorous but often impractical. None of these methods alone provides complete visibility or predictability. Instead, defenders must blend techniques carefully: use SBOMs to inform fuzz testing, apply fuzzing cautiously in controlled environments, and selectively use formal verification where specifications exist and stability can be assured. It's a careful balancing act, acknowledging that the ultimate nature of legacy software may never be fully understood.

Given these limitations, continuous behavior and communications monitoring become essential defensive strategies. Establishing clear operational baselines for normal protocol interactions enables security teams to quickly detect deviations or unexpected communications. Even without complete knowledge of a protocol's internal workings, anomalies—such as new devices appearing on the network, unexpected communication patterns, or abnormal command sequences—can provide critical early warnings. Proactive monitoring doesn't require perfect understanding; it demands vigilance and a readiness to respond swiftly when behavior diverges from established norms.

Real security for industrial protocols demands transparency by design: devices built from the ground up for visibility, formal modeling, and rigorous testing. It requires manufacturers to embrace openness not as a compliance burden but as an operational imperative. Until that cultural and technical shift occurs, defenders will continue to navigate uncertainty—armed only with partial insights and cautious interventions.

In the meantime, the best defense is awareness. Understanding the limits of our tools, recognizing the inherent uncertainty in legacy environments, and continually pushing for greater visibility wherever possible. Even imperfect visibility is better than none, and even limited understanding can inform better defenses. Legacy protocols may defy complete comprehension —but they need not defy defense entirely. Insecurity thrives in darkness, but even partial illumination, imperfect and incomplete, can be enough to hold the line until deeper reforms take root.

CHAPTER 21 –
GATEWAYS AND
GHOSTS: TRANSLATORS,
TRUST, AND TUNNELS

There's a quiet assumption that pervades industrial system design—an almost religious belief in the protective power of protocol boundaries. If a device speaks serial and the network is IP, then a gateway is placed in between. If an application needs data from a controller running an unfamiliar protocol, a translator is inserted to bridge the gap. Gateways are everywhere. They sit between fieldbuses and Ethernet, between vendor islands and supervisory systems, between PLCs and the historians that chart their every value. They're assumed to be passive, obedient, and protective. But like most assumptions in industrial security, the closer you examine them, the more fragile they become.

Gateways are not firewalls. They are interpreters. They receive data in one format, translate it, and transmit it in another. In many cases, they do this with no authentication, no encryption, and no awareness of context. A write command from an HMI in one protocol becomes a field command in another. A malformed packet from a vendor laptop becomes a control instruction. A spoofed Modbus request gets faithfully translated into a Profinet control action. The gateway does not ask questions. It just passes messages.

And in doing so, it often creates a false sense of security— an invisible tunnel between networks that are assumed to be segmented.

In industrial environments, protocol conversion is more than convenience—it's survival. Plants are built over decades, with equipment from multiple vendors, each using proprietary or domain-specific protocols. A single process area might contain Profibus field devices, Modbus/RTU controllers, Ethernet/IP supervisory links, and a central historian consuming OPC data. Without gateways, these systems would never speak. Gateways hold the patchwork together. But they also become bottlenecks of trust—critical junctions where data crosses domains, and where the integrity of communication is assumed, not verified.

The most dangerous gateways are the quietest ones—the ones that operate under the assumption that translation equals insulation. These devices are often treated like segmentation boundaries: the assumption is that what lies behind a Modbus-to-IP gateway is "air-gapped," or at least logically isolated. But the gateway itself is a live wire. If it accepts unauthenticated Modbus commands on its IP-facing interface, it will happily convert them to raw serial messages and send them downline. If it receives malformed packets, it may crash or reset. If it is misconfigured, it may forward traffic in both directions, opening paths for data exfiltration or command injection. The gateway becomes not a filter, but a bridge.

In one engagement, an attacker exploited this very behavior. A historian was connected to a SCADA system using OPC Classic. The SCADA server, in turn, communicated with a field PLC using Modbus/RTU via a serial-to-Ethernet gateway. The attacker gained access to the network segment hosting the historian—assumed to be low risk—and scanned for open ports. The gateway's IP interface responded on TCP 502. From there, the attacker issued Modbus commands directly to the PLC, wrapped in IP packets and routed through the translator. The plant operators never saw the attack coming. Their firewall logs showed nothing. Their SCADA system was untouched. The attack flowed through a pathway that was never supposed to exist.

These incidents are not rare. Many gateways operate with minimal configuration. They are installed to solve a functional problem—"we need to talk to that controller"—not to enforce a policy. Their configuration is rarely audited. Their firmware is rarely updated. They are often sourced from OEMs who treat protocol translation as an afterthought, or bundled into multi-function devices that blur the line between converter, switch, and router.

And gateways are not neutral. In many cases, the act of translation introduces ambiguity, or outright loss. Protocols like Modbus and Profinet have different notions of addressing, data typing, and command structure. A floating-point value in Profinet might require two Modbus registers and careful byte-ordering, but a misconfigured gateway might treat it as a 16-bit integer and truncate the value. OPC UA's structured data model can't be easily collapsed into Modbus's flat memory map without discarding metadata. Alarm states, diagnostics, and control logic can be distorted in the translation—resulting in silent loss of precision, context, or command intent. In complex systems, this distortion cascades. A translated value that's slightly wrong may not trigger an alarm, but it can nudge a process outside of safe limits.

Some modern gateways introduce security features—TLS wrappers, IP whitelisting, protocol filtering—but these features are often disabled by default. Operators are wary of anything that might disrupt timing, and many industrial protocols are intolerant of latency. As a result, the security benefits are sacrificed for predictability. The gateway becomes another transparent device in the path, assumed to be safe because it's invisible.

Yet invisibility is what makes them dangerous. Gateways are often unmonitored. They don't produce logs. They aren't integrated into SIEMs. They sit outside the standard asset inventory, especially when installed by contractors or vendors during system expansion. A rogue device can impersonate a trusted gateway. A man-in-the-middle attack can swap packets before translation. And a compromised gateway can silently alter values in either direction, translating malice into process.

Threat actors understand the strategic value of gateways. In several state-sponsored intrusions, including components of the Industroyer malware toolkit, attackers built protocol-aware payloads that targeted intermediary devices—not operator consoles, but the translation layer between them and the substation infrastructure. Gateways, when overlooked, allow attackers to bypass detection and embed themselves deeply in process control. In APT campaigns, persistent access was maintained through translation devices that had never been configured with credentials, patched, or even properly inventoried. The gateway became the foothold—not the objective, but the entry point.

The problem is compounded when gateways are not even recognized as distinct devices. Many are embedded within multi-function platforms—edge computing nodes, remote terminal units, or communication servers. Their translation behavior is just one feature among many. This abstraction creates architectural blindness. Diagrams show a clean line from SCADA to PLC, with the implicit assumption of homogeneity. But inside that line lives a translator—a policyless entity that decides how data flows, what is preserved, and what is lost. And in many environments, no one owns it. IT doesn't see it as a network device. OT sees it as infrastructure. Vendors see it as an appliance. Responsibility is scattered.

This abstraction also fuels false confidence in protocol security. TLS termination at the gateway doesn't protect the fieldbus beyond it. Role-based access enforced on the upstream side vanishes when translated into a protocol with no concept of identity. Secure OPC UA communications can enter a gateway and emerge as plain Modbus writes, stripped of all context and protection. Firewalls happily permit "secure" traffic to a gateway IP without understanding that what follows is unauthenticated control traffic aimed at real-world equipment. The protection is superficial. The risk is structural.

Defending against BACnet threats requires a shift in how buildings are understood—not as passive structures, but as cyber-physical ecosystems with control surfaces as vulnerable as any firewall or database. Building management systems must be inventoried, mapped, and monitored like the critical infrastructure they are. BACnet traffic should be baselined, inspected, and constrained. Writable object commands should be logged. Protocol-aware firewalls must understand the structure of BACnet messages and enforce rules at the object and function level—not just IP and port.

Operationally, gateways are neglected for a reason. They work. They're low maintenance. They rarely fail. But that dependability creates complacency. OT teams may not realize the translation logic has been modified. IT teams may not even know it exists. Vendors may update firmware without documenting new behaviors or defaults. And in incident response, gateways become black holes. No NetFlow. No syslog. No packet capture. Translated packets arrive at devices with no attribution—no upstream IPs, no user tokens, no forensic trail. The attacker is erased in the conversion. The damage persists.

Addressing gateway risk requires more than disabling a few ports. It means treating gateways as first-class security objects. They must be inventoried, monitored, patched, and logged. Their configuration must be reviewed not just for function, but for trust boundaries. Protocol filtering should be enforced, not optional. Command injection should be rate-limited or blocked outright. Gateway traffic should be modeled as a separate zone in the network, with the same care given to firewall rules and access control as any critical endpoint.

More fundamentally, the presence of a gateway should never be taken as proof of segmentation. Just because a device speaks a different protocol does not mean it is isolated. Translation is not protection. Bridging is not control. And silence is not safety.

Gateways are enablers of communication, but also of compromise. They are ghosts in the network—unseen, unchallenged, and all too often, misunderstood.

CHAPTER 22 – THE SUPPORT PORTAL IS ALWAYS OPEN: REMOTE ACCESS AS A THREAT VECTOR

Every plant, every facility, every industrial site has them—those devices, services, and workstations that were installed not for control, but for convenience. Somewhere in the architecture, behind the historian or near the control room, there's a box that says "Vendor Support," "Remote Access," or "Dial In Engineering Station." Sometimes it's a VPN tunnel. Sometimes it's a TeamViewer session. Sometimes it's a persistent Windows RDP port, configured during commissioning and forgotten the moment production began. It exists because systems break. Equipment needs updates. Experts need access. And when they're thousands of miles away, the quickest fix isn't a support contract—it's a persistent tunnel to the heart of the operation.

Remote access is not an edge case. It is embedded into the daily rhythm of industrial operations. When a PLC needs a patch, the vendor logs in. When a logic error appears during startup, the integrator connects to debug it. When the SCADA system throws an obscure fault, the manufacturer sends a technician—but not physically. Not anymore. They connect through a support portal—one that was supposed to be temporary. One that was supposed to be closed. One that nobody remembered was still open.

These access pathways are not theoretical. They are real, persistent, and dangerous. In the majority of post-incident reviews across industrial cyberattacks, remote access emerges not as an anomaly, but as the primary vector. It's not surprising. Remote access systems are convenient, powerful, and often invisible to security monitoring. They bypass physical boundaries. They neutralize air gaps. And in many architectures, they traverse layers of the Purdue Model without restriction, landing directly in Level 2 or Level 1, where control logic resides.

The attack surface varies. In some sites, the pathway is a standard IT VPN client installed on an engineering workstation. The credentials may be stored in the browser. The endpoint may be a shared PC used by multiple technicians. The VPN terminates inside the OT enclave, often with flat routing to control subnets. Once connected, the support team—or anyone who steals their credentials—has full access to control devices.

In other environments, the remote access point is a dedicated box—a cellular modem, an edge gateway, or a vendor-installed appliance. These are often deployed with little to no hardening. Default credentials persist. Firmware updates are rare. And visibility into their activity is limited or non-existent. The device may not log access attempts. It may not enforce timeouts. It may run an embedded web server that has never seen a penetration test.

TeamViewer, LogMeIn, and VNC are common. They're easy to deploy, cost nothing, and require no IT configuration. A technician installs them, shares an ID and password, and the vendor logs in at will. There's no firewall exception because the client initiates outbound connections. There's no SIEM alert because the traffic looks like any other web session. And there's no monitoring because the plant isn't staffed 24/7 with security professionals. In one post-incident review, a TeamViewer session remained active for over 90 days after a project had closed. The remote user could log in, view HMI screens, and interact with live control panels. No one noticed.

Even the remote access tools themselves introduce additional risk through telemetry and background services. Many of these platforms maintain persistent connections to cloud brokers—sending device metadata, status beacons, and usage statistics to vendor infrastructure. This creates new attack surfaces. If the vendor platform is compromised, the attacker gains insight into connected clients. Worse, actions taken through cloud-linked consoles may bypass local logging entirely. The plant may have no record of what was done. The vendor may have no idea who used the credentials.

The most insidious form of remote access isn't persistent—it's periodic. Some systems are designed to open a tunnel only when needed, via call-in request or heartbeat polling. These "on-demand" connections are marketed as secure alternatives. But they depend on secure implementation, access control, and human discipline. In one case, a vendor platform used HTTPS polling to check for support requests. But the poll included embedded credentials and a static session token. Once intercepted, the attacker could spoof the vendor, activate a tunnel, and gain access to the OT environment—without raising alarms.

Shadow IT further complicates the picture. Remote access is often established outside formal channels—by field engineers during commissioning, by third-party contractors during upgrades, or by in-house staff seeking a quick fix. USB cellular modems plugged into engineering workstations, remote desktop tools installed on unmanaged laptops, or rogue access points configured "just for testing" persist long after the original task is completed. In one plant, a field-deployed laptop was returned to inventory after diagnostics—but its stored VPN profile still connected to the OT gateway every time it was powered on.

Even when organizations attempt to secure access, contractual boundaries create blind spots. Many vendor agreements fail to specify how long remote access is valid, who owns credential rotation, or what happens when a support relationship ends. In regulated sectors, these gaps can be catastrophic. If a vendor credential is compromised and used to trigger an incident, liability may be unclear. The vendor may claim no active session was in progress. The plant may claim they didn't authorize the connection. And no one may have logs to prove what actually happened.

Worse still are multi-tenant remote access portals—vendor platforms designed to support many customers through a centralized dashboard. If an attacker compromises the vendor's administrative interface, they may gain access to dozens or hundreds of client environments in parallel. This is the supply chain at its most dangerous—not through malicious updates, but through shared, privileged visibility. A single portal breach can expose everything. Lateral movement isn't needed. The attacker simply clicks a dropdown.

And when compromise does happen, forensic visibility is often minimal. Remote sessions aren't recorded. Session histories are held by the vendor, not the client. Actions taken through legitimate access tools blend in with normal troubleshooting behavior. Command logs, if they exist at all, are fragmented across platforms. Even in post-incident analysis, defenders may be unable to determine whether the breach came from an insider, an attacker, or a third-party technician working under valid authorization.

The belief in air gaps continues to erode under this pressure. Many environments that are classified as isolated still contain remote access pathways—jump boxes with dual NICs, temporary vendor stations that were never decommissioned, or edge devices with cellular fallback that route to critical assets. These channels violate architectural assumptions. They bridge layers that were assumed to be sealed. And because they are often idle, they are invisible during routine scanning or audits.

There has to be a better way.

It is important to acknowledge that the chapter-opening line —"Every plant, every facility, every industrial site has them"—is impactful but not entirely accurate. While many environments have yielded to the convenience of persistent remote access, not all have. In fact, some refuse to compromise at all.

In certain critical infrastructure sectors—nuclear energy, weapons production, national defense, and classified government operations—remote access to the inner layers of the control network is strictly forbidden. These environments do not treat isolation as an architectural ideal—they enforce it as operational law. The two or three innermost rings of their defense-in-depth strategy are fully segregated. Communication into these zones is strictly one-way, usually via data diodes. Every connection, if permitted at all, is logged, monitored in real time, and subject to review.

When a vendor needs access in such environments, they must travel to the site in person. But they don't just show up. Physical access is highly controlled. In many cases, vendor laptops are prohibited entirely. If permitted, the devices must be submitted weeks in advance for extensive inspection, and they are often replaced by systems issued by the facility—pre-imaged, tightly restricted, and air-gapped by design. Portable media such as USB sticks or CDs must go through rigorous scanning using three to five anti-malware engines before data is transferred. The data is then written onto plant-issued media, tagged for a specific security level, and tracked throughout its lifecycle. Use of that media across zones is tightly restricted and closely monitored.

In one extreme example, a vendor was contracted to upgrade firmware on protected components located within a control room in a high-security critical infrastructure site. Remote access was not an option. There were no tunnels, no bridges, no digital conduits from the outside. Even physical entry to the control room was nontrivial—and the vendor's tools and lab infrastructure could not be brought inside. The solution was extraordinary: the vendor arrived with two tractor trailers containing a self-contained lab environment. Components were physically removed from the system, carried to the trailers for testing and upgrade, then returned, revalidated, and finally reconnected. No digital connection ever bridged the gap. The barrier held, not because of trust, but because of physical separation backed by policy and procedure.

These measures are considered extreme by most industry standards. But they demonstrate an essential truth: security is possible when architecture and discipline align. The presence of remote access is not a necessity—it is a design choice. And in environments where failure is intolerable, that choice is rejected outright. Control replaces convenience. Verification replaces assumption.

But, are these measures really extreme? Consider this context:

The product rolling off this manufacturer's line sells for between $50,000 and $100,000 per unit. The facility runs around the clock—24 hours a day, 365 days a year—both to satisfy the demand for the product and because downtime is prohibitively expensive. But precision is everything. If even a slight scratch or imperfection is found on a single unit, the response is immediate and severe. The manufacturer discards that flawed item along with the 20 that came before it and the 20 that followed—then shuts down the entire production line until the exact source of the defect is identified. The cost of one surface blemish can quickly spiral into millions of dollars in wasted inventory and lost uptime. In that kind of environment, where the margin for error is razor-thin and consequences multiply instantly, the idea of allowing remote access into control systems—just for convenience—feels less like a feature and more like a gamble no one can afford to lose.

The support portal is always open—not out of malice, but out of trust. And where trust is minimized, audited, and constrained by hardened boundaries, the risks it introduces can be managed. But if remote access exists at all, it must be considered a high-

BILL JOHNS

risk vector—and protected accordingly.

CHAPTER 23 – IN THE SERVICE MENU: BACKDOORS, MAINTENANCE MODES, AND FORGOTTEN FUNCTIONS

Every operator knows the public interface of a machine—the HMI screens, the control buttons, the alerts that flash during startup or shutdown. But beneath these familiar layers lies another world: a hidden interface meant not for control, but for correction. This is the service menu. The maintenance port. The configuration jumper. The undocumented command. These functions weren't designed for security. They were designed to help someone in a lab, or a factory, or a plant floor bring a system back online when something went wrong. And they're still there—unchanged, unmonitored, and often unknown to the defenders charged with securing the system decades later.

In the world of industrial control systems, the service menu is not a metaphor. Devices ship with diagnostics. Controllers have engineering modes. Field devices support configuration screens that unlock with obscure keypresses or DIP switch sequences. Many PLCs can be placed into a programming mode—often without authentication—allowing new logic to be uploaded directly to the processor. Some equipment includes hardcoded backdoors intended for factory use only, accessible through undocumented telnet or serial commands. These features are not bugs. They're support infrastructure. But in the hands of an attacker, they become control surfaces.

The problem is not just that these functions exist. It's that they're often forgotten. During commissioning, a technician may enable a feature to simplify troubleshooting—a console port, a debug log, an override jumper. Over time, the system is brought online, the device is left in place, and the temporary feature becomes permanent. The button labeled "maintenance" becomes part of normal operation. The jumper that allows firmware rollback stays bridged. And because these features are rarely visible to SCADA or central logging systems, they remain in the dark—until someone decides to use them.

Attackers have learned to look for these paths. In targeted campaigns, threat actors have issued control commands that are only accepted in engineering or service mode—bypassing user authentication and triggering firmware modification routines. In some environments, specific byte sequences sent over a serial connection can unlock manufacturer diagnostics, allowing raw memory access or parameter edits. In others, file uploads to a specific directory trigger device reconfiguration—because the system was never told not to trust them. These behaviors often bypass normal control channels entirely. They operate below the HMI, below the network, and sometimes below the awareness of the engineers maintaining the plant.

Many legacy systems don't support modern authentication at all. Access to the service menu may require nothing more than physical proximity or an open management port. In one well-documented case, a high-voltage breaker controller used a magnetic stylus to change states through a touchscreen interface. No passwords. No logs. If you knew how the menu worked, you could reconfigure the device in seconds. In another, a building automation system responded to a proprietary IR remote that activated engineering functions silently—without ever showing them on the screen.

Service menus are also embedded in protocol logic. DNP3 supports "direct operate" commands that can bypass confirmation routines. Modbus allows force-coil or force-register commands that override local control. S7Comm supports session establishment using functions intended for engineering software. These aren't vulnerabilities—they're features. But in flat networks, with poor segmentation and weak monitoring, they become open doors.

Sometimes, the danger lies not in the feature, but in how it behaves under stress. Devices enter safe mode, fallback mode, or local override mode after communication failures. In these modes, access control may be relaxed. Commands that would normally be rejected are now accepted. Timers are extended. Firmware protections are suspended. And unless you're watching for that state transition—unless you know that the device has moved from normal to degraded mode—you'll never know it's vulnerable.

Even devices that support encryption or authentication often leave the service channel untouched. The main interface may be hardened—passwords, certificates, TLS—but the out-of-band interface, the serial port, the vendor web GUI, remains unchanged. And because these access paths are rarely used, they're rarely tested. Vulnerabilities persist across firmware versions. Patches may not be issued, or may not be applied, because no one remembers what the service port is for.

In some cases, the vendor knows the access path exists—but won't disclose it. They classify it as a factory function. They require NDAs to discuss it. Or they embed the credentials in software used only by field technicians. But attackers don't need to ask. They can reverse-engineer the firmware. They can extract the secrets from memory dumps. And once the path is known, it applies across all deployed systems of that model—because these functions are rarely configurable.

These aren't just hypotheticals. Several high-profile cases have demonstrated how service menus, maintenance functions, and undocumented features have been exploited in the wild—or discovered accidentally, long after deployment.

One well-known example involved Schneider Electric's Modicon PLCs, widely used in water, manufacturing, and energy sectors. Security researchers discovered a hardcoded credential used in the web server interface for remote diagnostics. This credential allowed administrative access to the device—granting the ability to modify configuration files, download memory, or upload arbitrary firmware. The account was intended for support engineers but was never documented for customers. When the backdoor was uncovered and publicly disclosed, it forced a wide recall and spurred regulatory discussions about the acceptability of hardcoded service credentials in critical infrastructure.

In another case, Siemens S7-1200 and S7-1500 PLCs—devices heavily deployed in automation systems—were found to support session hijacking and insecure engineering protocol behaviors. While Siemens had introduced protection mechanisms through TIA Portal and secure communication channels, the underlying S7Comm protocol could still be abused if the attacker had access to the network. Tools like Snap7 and PLCScan could identify devices, extract project metadata, and replay control logic uploads—all without triggering alarms, if proper access control wasn't configured. These actions didn't require vulnerabilities—they were inherent in the way service interactions had been designed for convenience.

And in a dramatic real-world red team operation conducted against a critical manufacturing facility, the attackers gained access to an unused engineering workstation on the OT floor. The machine was connected via serial cable to multiple legacy relay controllers—each configured to allow ladder logic changes without authentication if placed in a physical maintenance state. By sending a series of timing pulses over the serial interface—something only known to field engineers or reverse engineers—the red team was able to rewrite control logic on live equipment. The PLCs never logged the activity. The workstation never showed an alert. And the changes remained in place even after power cycling. Only a deep manual inspection of the logic exposed the tampering, and by then, hours had passed.

Sometimes, these backdoors are stumbled upon by accident. In the case of Tridium's Niagara Framework, used in many building automation systems, researchers discovered that an undocumented admin panel could be accessed through a specific combination of web interface calls—unlocking debugging tools that were supposed to be available only during manufacturing. The tools allowed remote control of BACnet and Modbus endpoints—effectively giving attackers a control interface across building systems if the port was exposed. And in many installations, it was.

These case studies reveal a common pattern: the service menu is not simply a risk; it is a behavioral blind spot. Vendors build them for themselves. Integrators leave them behind. Operators don't know they exist. And attackers, with patience and knowledge, find them—not because they're breaking the system, but because they're using it exactly as it was designed, just not for the reasons it was intended.

Defending against the service menu is difficult because it's not a single thing. It's not a port you can block or a process you can kill. It's an entire class of behavior—emergent, undocumented, and hidden in the seams between engineering and operations. These paths often don't appear in manuals. They aren't captured in asset inventories. And because they're not part of routine monitoring, they evade detection unless you know where to look.

That's why the response must start with documentation. Every device must be interrogated—not just for its visible functions, but for what it *can* do under the right conditions. What protocols does it support? What interfaces are enabled at boot?

What does it do when you send malformed commands, or when the network goes dark? How does it behave when the firmware is corrupted, or when voltage levels drop? These are not academic questions. They define the perimeter—not the logical perimeter, but the functional one.

Mitigations must also be physical. If a port is never used, it must be disabled—physically, not just through software. If a jumper enables engineering mode, it must be removed or sealed. If a remote protocol supports configuration changes, those commands must be blocked at the network level—even if the vendor says they're safe. And if a device cannot be secured, it must be isolated. Air-gapped. Firewalled. Or replaced.

Defenders must also demand change from vendors. Service paths must be disclosed. Hardcoded credentials must be eliminated. Factory features must be documented, controlled, and made configurable by the asset owner. And firmware updates must address—not preserve—legacy behavior. Transparency cannot be optional. Because when a vendor builds a secret into your system, they've made a decision on your behalf. And that decision may open the door to compromise.

Most of all, defenders must stop assuming that what's visible is what's vulnerable. The real danger may live in the unexamined layers—beneath the HMI, behind the panel, or inside the service menu that no one has touched in years. Because attackers don't care what the user manual says. They're already pressing buttons you've forgotten exist.

PART IV
Strategic Tensions and Converged Defenses

CHAPTER 24 - NATION-STATE INTEREST IN PROTOCOL EXPLOITATION

At some point, the rules changed. Protocols were never meant to be weapons. They were mechanisms for cooperation, for repeatability, for control. But over time, those mechanisms became predictable enough to manipulate, and complex enough to subvert. What started as trusted communications evolved into strategic targets—because when you understand how something speaks, you don't need to break it to control it. You just need to talk better than the person who owns it.

The shift wasn't immediate. Early malware in industrial environments was blunt, opportunistic. It didn't understand what it was talking to. It simply ran scripts, copied files, disrupted processes. But beginning around 2010, a new pattern emerged: malware that was protocol-aware, context-sensitive, and operationally precise. These weren't generic payloads—they were engineered campaigns that learned to speak the language of the industrial process itself. And they didn't always exploit vulnerabilities in the conventional sense. They exploited assumptions—assumptions of trust, behavior, and default design.

Stuxnet was the first. It didn't just infect industrial systems. It modeled them. It knew the exact version of Siemens Step 7 it needed. It injected itself into the PLC upload cycle, quietly modifying logic on the controller while leaving the engineering workstation untouched. There was no buffer overflow or code injection in the target protocol. It used valid instructions. It used the protocol as it was meant to be used—just for a different purpose. The sophistication was not in its code, but in its fidelity. It understood how centrifuge cascades operated. It knew what speed to run at, and for how long. And when it needed to hide, it intercepted telemetry and fed the operators false data. The protocol was the canvas. The attack was a brushstroke hidden in plain sight.

Stuxnet didn't compromise the control system by breaking the software. It compromised it by impersonating the operator. It leveraged protocol knowledge to inject commands that looked legitimate. The PLCs received valid instructions from a trusted source, over a trusted channel, in a trusted format. No alarms were raised, because nothing was technically wrong. But trust itself was the vulnerability. Once breached, the system had no immune response.

What made the attack even more insidious was how little resistance the protocol offered. Most industrial control protocols —Modbus, DNP3, IEC 104—lack native authentication or session management. There are no login prompts, no encryption handshakes, no sequence tracking. If you speak the right function code, the device listens. There's no difference between a legitimate operator and malicious software pretending to be one. The protocols trust the network, and the network trusts the sender. It's obedience by design.

Other actors paid attention. If Stuxnet had been a surgical strike, Industroyer was a tactical lesson in system-wide sabotage. Discovered in Ukraine in 2016, it was one of the first public examples of malware built explicitly to interact with power grid components using legitimate industrial protocols. IEC 60870-5-101, IEC 104, OPC Classic, and even standard Windows APIs were all leveraged—not to exploit software bugs, but to control switches, breakers, and relays. The attackers didn't need rootkits. They needed runtime access and protocol fluency.

Industroyer used protocol stacks to do exactly what they were designed to do: send commands, receive responses, and coordinate system behavior. Its power came from that simplicity. It didn't break the system—it became part of it. It spoke like a SCADA master. It issued trip commands. It altered configurations. It waited. In some cases, it rewrote firmware in field devices to prevent recovery. Not because it had to, but because it could. The protocols didn't stop it. They enabled it.

But Industroyer didn't come out of nowhere. Before it, there was GreyEnergy—a quieter, longer campaign that laid the groundwork. Between 2015 and 2018, it infiltrated multiple energy sector networks in Ukraine and Poland, not to trip breakers, but to observe how they worked. Its tools harvested control system documentation, protocol configurations, and relay logic—preparing for a moment when protocol fluency would become action. It was a reconnaissance campaign designed not to disable systems, but to understand them deeply enough to do so later, with surgical precision. GreyEnergy wasn't designed to break infrastructure—it was designed to map it, so the next attacker wouldn't have to.

The same logic played out in the TRISIS malware discovered at a petrochemical plant in Saudi Arabia in 2017. TRISIS, also known as TRITON, was designed to compromise safety instrumented systems—specifically, Schneider Electric's Triconex controllers. These weren't standard PLCs. They were safety systems engineered to take control when everything else failed. But like everything else, they communicated over a protocol. TRISIS inserted itself into that communication path.

The malware didn't use an exploit to breach the SIS controller. It used the TriStation protocol, a proprietary interface intended for engineering configuration and diagnostics. The attackers had reverse-engineered it—despite limited documentation and proprietary encoding—to craft messages that mimicked a technician's commands. They used those messages to inject code, disable safety logic, and prepare the controller to allow unsafe conditions to persist undetected. The protocol didn't protect the controller. It welcomed the attacker, believing it was speaking to a trusted engineer.

In all these cases—Stuxnet, Industroyer, GreyEnergy, TRISIS— the attackers often used zero-day vulnerabilities to gain initial access, escalate privileges, or move laterally within Windows environments. But the real operational advantage didn't come from breaking systems open. It came from knowing how to manipulate them from the inside. Once access was obtained, the final payloads relied not on memory corruption or kernel exploits, but on deep protocol fluency. The malware issued trusted messages, used documented commands, and behaved like an operator. The vulnerability wasn't just in software. It was in trust.

This shift redefined how nation-states and advanced persistent threat actors approached industrial networks. Protocols were no longer background utilities. They were foreground targets. Intelligence services began mapping control systems not by IP ranges, but by protocol versions and vendor fingerprints. Red teams trained on ladder logic, on GOOSE messaging, on Siemens S7 and GE SRTP. Tools emerged to enumerate field devices by speaking their native dialects. Malware kits began including protocol modules—not exploits, but fully compliant stacks, capable of integrating silently into industrial environments and issuing commands without detection.

The trend didn't stop with the so-called big three. In 2021, U.S. intelligence sources disclosed PIPESTALK—a campaign targeting gas pipeline infrastructure. The goal wasn't disruption. It was comprehension. The intrusions focused on SCADA polling intervals, Modbus command patterns, and compressor station logic. These were nation-state actors documenting protocol structure, not exploiting it—yet. The message was clear: the protocol wasn't just a means of communication. It was the target.

In Ukraine again, during the 2022 escalation, Russian actors deployed a new variant: Industroyer2. It was smaller than its predecessor. Tighter. More efficient. It didn't need elaborate frameworks. It issued IEC 104 messages with precision—enough to trip switches and darken substations. It didn't scan or probe. It acted. It relied on the same trust assumptions as its predecessor, and they still worked.

As electrical substations modernized, attackers adapted. In 2022, researchers observed early-stage malware called ParasiteLoader that targeted GOOSE messages in IEC 61850 systems—used to issue protection signals between digital relays. By spoofing multicast messages or disrupting the timing required for proper failover, the malware could desynchronize protective systems, potentially preventing them from responding to faults. This wasn't just about tripping relays. It was about manipulating the heartbeat of digital protection itself—using protocol fluency as a weapon.

Even when defenders capture protocol traffic, they rarely inspect it. Industrial protocols are often excluded from SIEM ingestion due to cost or complexity. Many DPI tools don't understand protocol nuance, and those that do are misconfigured or overwhelmed by noise. A Modbus write is seen as routine. A DNP3 trip message is logged as telemetry. Security teams trained in TCP/IP stacks and Windows logs don't look for sabotage in function code 5 or 43. The attackers know this. They rely on it.

And increasingly, the attackers aren't just issuing commands —they're using industrial protocols as camouflage. The Snake malware, attributed to Russia's Turla group, exemplified this trend. In variants observed in defense-linked infrastructure, C2 traffic was encapsulated inside payloads that mimicked ICS telemetry. Firewalls permitted it. Monitoring tools ignored it. The protocol wasn't just a vector. It was a disguise.

These operations were not smash-and-grab. They were dwell-

and-decide. The malware lived in systems for months or years, collecting data, learning patterns, and waiting for a signal. When the signal came, it didn't break windows. It opened doors. It tripped switches. It sent perfectly valid messages with perfectly timed payloads, and the systems obeyed—because protocol logic doesn't question intent. It executes.

Protocol exploitation doesn't look like a breach. It looks like control.

The next wave of protocol exploitation may not even require human reverse engineering. AI-assisted tools now exist that can learn ICS behavior, identify command-response logic, and simulate operator activity in days, not months. Malware is being modularized. Operators can load protocol drivers like plug-ins, selecting from a library of known dialects to match their target. Autonomous protocol fuzzers are emerging in military and contractor labs. The bar for speaking "ICS" has dropped—not because the protocols got simpler, but because learning them has become automated.

The lesson of the last decade is not that protocols are weak—it's that they are too trusted. They are gates left open not by failure, but by design. Nation-state adversaries have learned to walk through those gates, not with exploits or force, but with fluency. And until defenders learn to scrutinize protocol behavior as closely as they inspect binaries or firewalls, the most powerful tools in the system will remain its most vulnerable.

CHAPTER 25 - PROTOCOL ADAPTATION AND PSEUDO-SECURITY

The industrial world is full of wrappers. Tunnels, gateways, overlays, and encrypted proxies—each promising to make old protocols safe in a modern world. They are sold as upgrades, deployed as fixes, and advertised as proof that the past doesn't need to be replaced, only shielded. But beneath these layers of retrofitted security lies a simple truth: you can encrypt a protocol without making it trustworthy. You can tunnel it without making it safe. And you can protect its transport while still allowing it to do dangerous things.

This is the era of pseudo-security. Not because the intentions are bad, but because the foundations are brittle. Industrial protocols like Modbus, DNP3, and OPC were never designed with adversaries in mind. They were meant for trusted networks, physical isolation, and cooperative nodes. They assumed that if you could speak the protocol, you were authorized to speak it. There was no authentication, no role enforcement, no transaction validation. The goal was interoperability, not resilience. And once that trust model was broken, the security model collapsed with it.

The rise of encryption wrappers wasn't driven by security ambition. It was driven by necessity. As compliance pressures mounted and auditors began asking hard questions about remote access and visibility, operators looked for the fastest way to protect data in transit without ripping out legacy control systems. Wrapping a protocol in a tunnel became the easiest way to check a box without reengineering the plant. It was triage masquerading as strategy.

Rather than redesign these protocols from the ground up, many vendors chose a different path: wrap the existing protocol in a secure channel, and hope that was enough. The most common adaptation is the tunnel—encrypt the traffic using TLS or IPsec and run the insecure protocol inside. On the surface, this adds confidentiality. It prevents casual interception. It may even provide client authentication via certificates or keys. But it doesn't fix the protocol itself. The commands inside the tunnel are still unauthenticated. The function codes still assume trust. And the devices still respond to anything that looks well-formed.

VPN overlays are a popular example. A vendor may recommend that Modbus traffic be routed through a site-to-site VPN, encrypting the data between locations. This hides the traffic from observers, but it doesn't protect the end systems. Once inside the tunnel, a rogue device can issue any Modbus command it likes. If it knows the address and the function code, the system will respond. There's no application-layer check, no identity, no enforcement. The VPN was meant to protect the transport, not the logic. And in doing so, it often provides a false sense of security—especially when vendors call it "end-to-end encrypted control."

The Colonial Pipeline attack in 2021 brought this issue into sharp relief. Attackers didn't need to break a protocol or reverse-engineer a fieldbus. They simply acquired a single VPN credential—valid and trusted—and used it to access internal systems. Inside the tunnel, everything was assumed safe. Devices and services trusted any client that had crossed the VPN boundary. There was no revalidation, no protocol awareness, no scrutiny. A single login became a master key. The attack didn't exploit Modbus or OPC directly—it exploited the idea that anything in the tunnel must be legitimate.

One recurring mistake in pseudo-secure environments is treating encryption as a control boundary. A device behind a VPN isn't isolated—it's just encrypted. TLS doesn't restrict what can be said. It only hides who is saying it. Without true policy enforcement, encryption becomes a velvet rope for attackers: soft to cross, and inviting once breached.

Other adaptations use protocol gateways—devices or software proxies that translate between insecure and more modern dialects. A gateway might take inbound Modbus over TCP and expose it as OPC UA on the internal side. Or vice versa. These gateways sometimes add basic access controls, whitelisting certain commands or registers. But more often, they simply repackage the protocol in a different format. The underlying permissions, assumptions, and behaviors remain the same. Worse, gateways can introduce new problems—like mismatched timeouts, conversion bugs, or broken state tracking between layers.

Some environments have attempted to modernize insecure protocols by funneling them through middleware: brokers, pub/sub buses, or translation layers. These systems are often deployed for scalability, not security. But when they become the central conduit for protocol interaction, they introduce a new risk: compromise of the broker is compromise of the process. If the middleware lacks protocol validation or role enforcement, it becomes an insecure clearinghouse—disguised as modernization.

Then there are the so-called "secure versions" of legacy protocols. Secure DNP3 is one example. It adds message authentication, sequence numbers, and optional encryption to the base DNP3 protocol. On paper, it's a major improvement. It prevents spoofing, detects replay attacks, and ensures integrity. But in practice, Secure DNP3 is rarely deployed. It requires compatible implementations on both ends, certificate management, and configuration changes that many asset owners avoid. In most environments where DNP3 is used, the secure version remains disabled. Devices may support it, but networks don't enable it. The protocol is secure in theory, but plaintext in practice.

Even where cryptographic protections exist, they often fail in execution. Certificate expiration halts communication until manual intervention. Trust hierarchies are misconfigured. Devices are deployed with certificate pinning disabled or with "trust all" flags set to avoid integration issues. The presence of encryption is not evidence of trust—it is evidence of an opportunity to trust. And too often, that opportunity is squandered.

OPC UA was supposed to be a clean break—a modern, secure, extensible version of the aging OPC Classic framework. It uses structured data, supports encryption and authentication, and runs over well-defined transport layers. But even OPC UA inherits some of the problems it was meant to fix. Implementations vary widely. Some vendors disable security features for convenience. Others configure OPC UA to trust all client certificates by default. And because the protocol is complex, security teams often don't inspect the traffic at all. It's opaque, dynamic, and misunderstood. The result is a system that may be secure at the transport layer, but fragile and permissive at the application layer.

Even worse, many OPC UA implementations ship with the so-called "None" security profile enabled by default. This means no encryption, no message signing, and no authentication. In many cases, this is the only mode in which client-server interoperability works out of the box. Operators, faced with tight schedules and integration headaches, leave it that way. Security exists in the protocol spec, but not in the field.

One of the most dangerous misconceptions in industrial security is that encryption enforces authorization. It doesn't. TLS verifies who you are—not what you're allowed to do. A properly encrypted session can still carry unauthorized commands, because the protocol itself doesn't care. Once inside the tunnel, the message is treated as trusted. The question isn't whether the message is secure. It's whether the system should listen.

In many field devices, protocol stacks are not modular. Modbus, DNP3, and vendor-specific interfaces often coexist in tight, interdependent firmware. Attempting to harden one interface can trigger unpredictable behavior in another. Even small changes—like adding message signing—can cause cascading failures in buffer allocation, timing, or interrupt handling. The legacy software ecosystem is fragile by nature, and securing it requires intimate knowledge of its dependencies, not just its interfaces.

The core issue with these adaptations isn't that they're useless. It's that they're incomplete. They protect data in motion, but not in meaning. They ensure that no one can read your Modbus message in transit—but do nothing to stop a rogue client from writing to a coil. They encrypt DNP3 commands—but not the logic that decides whether a command should be honored. They wrap dangerous functionality in a secure envelope and call it safe.

This approach creates systemic blindness. Security reviews focus on tunnel strength, key rotation, cipher selection. But they ignore what the protocol is actually doing. Is the command allowed? Is the device in the right state to receive it? Should that request even exist on this interface? These questions go unanswered, because the assumption is that if the transport is secure, the content must be trusted. It's the same logic that makes people feel safe behind locked doors, even when the person with the key is the threat.

Pseudo-security also obscures responsibility. Vendors can claim their devices are "secure" because they support TLS. Operators believe their environment is protected because they use a VPN. Auditors see encryption and check the box. But none of this speaks to the intent, safety, or correctness of the protocol interactions themselves. The system is "secure" in a way that is deeply disconnected from the risks it faces. The hard questions —about access control, safety boundaries, privilege separation —are pushed aside in favor of superficial protections that look good on paper.

None of this is to suggest that tunnels, proxies, and encryption should be abandoned. In the world we have—not the one we want—these wrappers are often the best tools we have to contain legacy risk. When combined with network isolation, layered defenses, strong segmentation, and micro-segmentation, they create meaningful friction for attackers. They help enforce containment, reduce lateral movement, and shield fragile devices from exposure. These controls matter. They should be deployed widely and maintained rigorously. But they must be deployed with a clear understanding: what they are protecting remains inherently insecure. They buy time. They don't solve the core problem.

Worse, attempts to "fix" insecure protocols by modifying device behavior or injecting untested security controls into running environments can be dangerous. Industrial systems are sensitive to timing, to packet structure, to communication frequency. Changing the behavior of a protocol stack without a complete understanding of its operational impact can break functionality—or, in critical cases, compromise safety. In these environments, the cost of good intentions can be high. Which is why compensating controls must be used thoughtfully, consistently, and with full awareness of what they can and cannot do.

While the protocols themselves may be flawed, defenders are not powerless. Even insecure or legacy protocols can be made observable. When traffic is monitored continuously, profiled for behavioral norms, and analyzed for out-of-band activity, even stateless protocols begin to reveal patterns. A rogue write command. An unauthorized client. A message issued at the wrong time of day, to the wrong device, with the wrong function code. These are not vulnerabilities. They are anomalies —detectable, if someone is looking.

Constant monitoring is not just important—it is imperative. In environments where you cannot patch, replace, or re-engineer protocol logic, you must watch it. That means deep packet inspection that understands industrial protocols. It means baselining expected communications and alerting on deviations. It means not just logging events, but understanding what those events mean. When two devices suddenly start speaking outside of maintenance windows—or a new master device appears on the bus—that may be the only warning you get.

Vulnerability management in OT doesn't stop at CVEs. It begins with visibility. You cannot defend what you don't understand. Knowing what protocol is in use is not the same as knowing what it's doing, or why, or whether it should. Most attacks don't rely on exotic flaws. They rely on trusted protocols doing unexpected things, unnoticed.

This is where pseudo-security can be countered with real security practices. Wrapping a protocol may hide it. But monitoring reveals it. Encryption may secure the message in transit, but vigilance secures the system in operation.

Protocol wrapping is not wrong. It's incomplete. It's a temporary bridge across a foundational flaw. And like any bridge, it should be crossed with caution, maintained with vigilance, and eventually replaced with something stronger.

Real security demands more than encryption. It demands protocol-level introspection. It requires systems that ask not just who sent a message, but should that message be sent at all. It requires function codes that enforce roles, registers that resist tampering, and devices that challenge assumptions. Wrapping a legacy protocol in a secure tunnel doesn't make it modern. It makes it silent and obedient—until the wrong command slips through.

There are better models. Protocol-aware firewalls can inspect industrial traffic and enforce intent. Token-based access systems can prevent unauthorized commands, even over trusted channels. Message signing can ensure integrity at the application layer, not just the transport. These are harder problems to solve—but they speak to the heart of the issue: security must be baked into the protocol itself, not laminated onto its surface.

Until that shift happens, the industry will remain in a dangerous equilibrium. Devices will speak insecure languages inside secure tunnels. Networks will trust what they cannot verify. And attackers—once inside—will find a landscape of perfectly encrypted pathways leading straight to unguarded logic.

CHAPTER 26 - DESIGNING PROTOCOLS FOR ADVERSARIAL ENVIRONMENTS

In the industrial world, the environment is not only physical but adversarial. This is the foundational failure of most operational technology (OT) protocol design efforts to date: they assume a cooperative world. Their creators built them to function, not to withstand compromise. These protocols were engineered to be lightweight, deterministic, and efficient—not resilient under attack. Their operational assumptions favored openness over obfuscation, convenience over confidentiality, and trust over verification. This chapter asks a simple question: what would it look like if we built OT protocols for the world we live in now—a world where compromise is not just possible, but expected?

The historical context for most OT protocols stretches back to the 1970s and 1980s, when proprietary fieldbus networks and serial communications were the norm. In that era, the dominant concern was interoperability between programmable logic controllers (PLCs), remote terminal units (RTUs), and supervisory systems. Engineers weren't concerned about man-in-the-middle attacks or lateral movement by hostile actors. The worst they expected was accidental disruption, not malicious intent. Protocols like Modbus, DNP3, and Profibus were therefore built with a design ethos that assumed physical control of the plant floor, physical access to the network, and good-faith interactions between trusted systems.

But as we know now, that model no longer holds.

One of the clearest wake-up calls came not from the OT space, but from the broader IT world. The transition from insecure to secure transport protocols across enterprise systems—such as from HTTP to HTTPS, telnet to SSH, or FTP to SFTP—was driven by the realization that networks could not be trusted. The internet was hostile terrain. Users were no longer inside controlled LANs—data traveled across unknown and often compromised routes. This led to the wholesale rethinking of how two systems verify each other's identity, negotiate trust, and protect session integrity. Cryptography became the default posture. But this was not simply a matter of encrypting data in transit. It required a complete reevaluation of trust models, session establishment, and identity validation.

The OT world, by contrast, largely remained unchanged. Even today, many industrial environments continue to rely on unauthenticated, unencrypted communications over networks that are increasingly exposed to both internal and external threats. Modbus/TCP continues to send control commands in plaintext, while legacy DNP3 implementations accept unsolicited messages from any device capable of forming a valid packet. In many of these networks, anyone who can reach the port can issue a command. And as the attack surface grows, that "anyone" is no longer a theoretical concern.

The 2015 and 2016 Ukraine grid attacks serve as case studies in what happens when protocol design fails to account for hostile actors. In both instances, attackers breached the IT networks of regional power distribution companies, pivoted into the OT environment, and issued valid control commands to substation equipment. They didn't exploit esoteric bugs or rely on zero-days. Instead, they used the protocols exactly as intended—issuing commands through legitimate interfaces that lacked any meaningful form of authentication. The protocols functioned flawlessly, but they did so in the service of adversaries.

This illustrates why secure channel negotiation must be treated as foundational. Protecting payloads is not enough; the communication session itself must be authenticated, encrypted, and tamper-proof from the outset. This requires mutual authentication embedded in the protocol handshake and not left to vendor-specific implementations or post-hoc configurations. Modern secure communication frameworks like mutual TLS accomplish this by requiring both sides of a session to verify digital certificates before any meaningful data is exchanged. In OT environments, however, such mechanisms are rarely implemented and even more rarely enforced.

Efforts have been made. Secure DNP3, formally known as DNP3 Secure Authentication, introduces challenge–response mechanisms based on cryptographic hashes to validate control messages. While this is a step forward, it remains optional and inconsistently adopted. Many vendors still default to insecure modes, and asset owners often disable security features to maintain compatibility or reduce perceived complexity. As a result, attackers can simply bypass protections by interacting with legacy devices or falling back to insecure modes. This optionality undermines the entire effort. Protocol security must be default, mandatory, and consistently implemented across all devices.

A central tenet in this shift is the concept of cryptographic identity. In an adversarial environment, it is not enough for a device to say who it is—it must prove it. Identity in secure protocol design is not a label, but a cryptographic assertion. This means assigning each device a unique identity rooted in strong key material and supported by a trust infrastructure that enables revocation and renewal. The IEEE 802.1AR standard, for instance, provides a blueprint for device identity that can support secure enrollment and ongoing authentication. Crucially, these credentials must not be hardcoded, unchangeable, or hidden behind vendor secrecy. They must be visible, testable, and tied to tamper-resistant hardware modules when possible.

The dangers of neglecting this principle became painfully clear in the 2017 TRITON attack on a petrochemical plant in the Middle East. The attackers targeted the Schneider Electric Triconex Safety Instrumented System (SIS), modifying its configuration in ways that could have disabled physical safety mechanisms. While many details remain classified, forensic investigations confirmed that the attackers used legitimate engineering tools to communicate with the SIS controller. The protocol in use lacked strong authentication, and the trust model was entirely based on network placement and access assumptions. Had the protocol required signed logic updates or cryptographic session validation, the attack path might have been far more complex—or entirely blocked.

In hostile environments, trust is not just about identity but also about accountability. This is where non-repudiation becomes critical. Control systems need to know not just that a command was received, but who issued it, under what authority, and whether the command was altered in transit. Protocols designed for accountability must embed digital signatures into control messages, coupled with time-stamping and audit mechanisms that resist tampering. These logs become essential not just for forensics after an incident but also for real-time detection of anomalous behavior. Without verifiable logging and origin tracing, an attacker's actions can masquerade as legitimate operations, leaving defenders blind and uncertain.

The Stuxnet worm, which targeted Iranian uranium enrichment centrifuges at Natanz in 2010, offers a vivid example of the absence of such controls. The malware used stolen digital certificates to sign its payloads, ensuring it would be trusted by Windows systems and Siemens Step7 software alike. It then reprogrammed PLCs using standard control logic that passed through legitimate interfaces. The PLCs accepted the logic without challenge. No authentication was required. No verification was enforced. The result was the covert physical destruction of thousands of centrifuges. The lack of non-repudiation mechanisms allowed the worm to operate invisibly, impersonating trusted operators at every step.

Even more subtle forms of attack exploit another common design flaw in legacy protocols: fail-operational behavior. Most control systems are designed to continue operating under degraded conditions, which makes sense in a physical safety context. But in adversarial settings, this behavior can be exploited. Devices that continue executing commands in the absence of authentication or after a connection drop are effectively open to hijack. Protocols must be designed to fail securely, not merely fail operationally. That means refusing commands that cannot be verified, pausing execution when inputs are suspect, and requiring re-authentication after disconnection. Continuing operation under uncertain trust conditions is not a feature—it's a vulnerability.

This flaw was visible again in the 2021 Oldsmar, Florida, water treatment facility intrusion. An unknown actor gained remote access to the control system and attempted to increase the sodium hydroxide levels in the water supply to dangerous levels. While the attack was caught in time, the protocol stack in use—likely based on a mix of remote desktop protocols and insecure industrial communications—lacked any mechanism to verify whether the commands being issued were legitimate. The system trusted the input because it had no mechanism not to. In environments where physical safety is at stake, this is unacceptable.

Building resilient protocols also means designing with compromise in mind. Security cannot rely on the idea that the network is trusted or that access controls are perfect. Protocols must operate securely even when they are running on a hostile network, surrounded by potentially compromised devices. This requires features such as strict command validation, stateful tracking of interactions, cryptographic session controls, and behavioral expectations that can detect and respond to anomalies. Some newer architectures embed these features—for example, OPC UA over TLS, when implemented with rigorous policy enforcement and signed message exchange—but most real-world deployments remain partial, inconsistent, or too complex to manage effectively.

True resilience also requires that protocols be observable and testable. The complexity of many industrial protocols, combined with poor documentation and proprietary extensions, makes them difficult to audit or analyze. Protocols should be designed as finite-state machines with defined transitions, allowing formal verification, simulation, and robust fuzz testing. Without this visibility, defenders are left guessing how a protocol will behave under duress—or worse, learning through failure during a live incident.

Protocol design must also account for the full lifecycle of a device. This includes secure provisioning, enrollment into trust domains, routine credential renewal, software updates, and eventual decommissioning. Static credentials and immutable stacks are incompatible with long-term security. Instead, secure protocols must assume dynamism—rotating secrets, renewing trust, and supporting graceful, verifiable upgrade paths over the life of a device. These are not edge-case concerns; they are foundational to long-term resilience.

Ultimately, the industrial protocols of the future must abandon the assumption of trust and embrace the certainty of threat. The world has changed. The adversary is no longer theoretical. Protocols must be born in that reality—not retrofitted to survive it. Designing for an adversarial environment does not mean sacrificing performance or operational clarity. It means embedding security into the very logic that governs how machines speak to each other. Because in this new era, function is not enough. Trust must be earned, proven, and enforced at every step.

Let the next generation of protocols begin where the last

generation failed—with the recognition that resilience is not an add-on. It is the design.

CHAPTER 27 –
NEXT PROTOCOLS, SAME PROBLEMS: THE UNEVEN EVOLUTION OF SECURE COMMUNICATION

There was a time when simply switching protocols felt like a fix. When the industry finally acknowledged that legacy stacks like Modbus, DNP3, and BACnet were functionally blind to modern threats, it began to look elsewhere—for protocols born in a world where adversaries were assumed, not ignored. New designs were proposed, standards committees were convened, and vendors promised secure replacements. OPC UA would finally fix the sins of OPC Classic. Secure DNP3 would close the loop on trusted serial links gone IP. IEC 62351 would bring authentication and encryption to energy protocols. DDS, MQTT with TLS, even proprietary secure wrappers—all heralded as the future of safe industrial communication. But then reality caught up.

Upgrading protocols sounds simple on paper. But paper doesn't run the plant. In the real world, each protocol sits atop a complex lattice of firmware limitations, application logic, timing dependencies, and network behavior that has been tuned, retuned, and hardwired into infrastructure. The result is a paradox. We have newer, more secure protocols. We even have standards that describe how to deploy them securely. But they remain the exception, not the norm—relegated to pilot projects, vendor demos, and greenfield builds. The legacy protocols remain in charge. And the newer ones, even when deployed, often end up configured in ways that betray their potential.

Take OPC UA, arguably the most mature and widely adopted of the "next generation" protocols. Developed to correct the chaos of OPC Classic—which depended on Windows DCOM, dynamic ports, and privilege inheritance—OPC UA was built with security in mind from the start. It included certificate-based authentication, encrypted transport, message signing, and flexible user access controls. On paper, it was the antidote to protocol blindness. In practice, its adoption revealed a troubling pattern. When offered secure and insecure deployment modes, many integrators chose the latter—not out of malice, but convenience. Certificate management was unfamiliar. Enabling encryption sometimes introduced latency or broke compatibility with existing middleware. So in too many deployments, OPC UA became just another cleartext channel, running over TCP without its built-in protections engaged. A secure protocol, used insecurely, behaves no differently than an insecure one.

The same story repeats with Secure DNP3. Its original design was deeply flawed—unauthenticated, unauditable, and built for serial transport. Secure DNP3 aimed to fix that by layering in symmetric encryption, MACs (message authentication codes), and a handshake mechanism. But secure modes introduced overhead. They weren't backward-compatible. And more importantly, the cost of upgrading was high. Devices had to support it. Networks had to tolerate the timing changes. Operators had to configure it correctly. So in most environments, it was quietly ignored. Standard DNP3 persisted, even as attackers developed tools to manipulate it without tripping any alarms.

And then there is MQTT, a protocol not born in industrial circles, but rapidly adopted by them for IIoT applications. Its lightweight design and publish/subscribe model made it ideal for telemetry, analytics, and cloud-bound data aggregation. It was fast, flexible, and simple. But MQTT's simplicity is also its weakness. It offers no built-in security. No authentication. No encryption. Its designers assumed that those layers would be handled by the transport—typically via TLS or through broker-based authentication. But here too, misconfiguration reigns. MQTT brokers are often deployed with default credentials, open ports, and no client validation. In some cases, devices publish sensitive process variables to public cloud endpoints with no protections at all. Again, the protocol allows for security— but it does not enforce it. And in environments where uptime and ease-of-integration take precedence, enforcement rarely happens.

Even where secure protocols are mandated—by regulation, policy, or procurement—implementation gaps abound. IEC 62351, which outlines secure profiles for protocols like IEC 60870-5-104 and IEC 61850, is a prime example. It describes how to apply TLS, manage certificates, and enforce role-based access. But it is a sprawling standard, inconsistently interpreted by vendors and unevenly implemented across devices. Some support only partial subsets. Others implement deprecated cipher suites. Interoperability becomes a guessing game. Field deployments often reveal mismatched expectations between vendors, integrators, and operators. The result is a secure protocol ecosystem with broken guarantees—where security exists in theory, but fails in practice.

And even when these protocols are deployed, they rarely replace their insecure predecessors. OPC UA is often used *alongside* OPC Classic, not instead of it. Secure DNP3-capable devices are frequently configured to fall back to legacy mode to maintain compatibility with older SCADA systems. DDS deployments may rely on modern publish-subscribe mechanics, but still wrap insecure process logic carried forward from legacy designs. Protocol evolution has not meant protocol elimination —it has simply layered new languages atop the same brittle assumptions.

Ironically, some next-generation protocols introduce additional risks when their security features are misunderstood or partially implemented. Transport encryption with static, self-signed certificates that are never rotated. Authentication schemes that accept any client certificate as valid. Firewalls that allow encrypted traffic to pass unchecked because inspection is no longer possible. These implementations create an illusion of security while preserving the same underlying attack paths. Misconfigured security is often worse than no security—because it breeds false confidence, making defenders believe the problem has been solved.

The illusion is reinforced by the language used in vendor marketing and procurement processes. "Supports TLS." "Secure by design." "IEC 62443 compliant." These statements are almost never scrutinized for operational meaning. In practice, vendors deliver partial implementations—TLS without mutual authentication, access control that exists but isn't enforced, or certificate infrastructures with no revocation capability. Integrators, under pressure to deliver functionality quickly, often disable or ignore secure features to get systems online. The box is checked. The protocol is "secured." The deployment, in reality, is wide open.

And even when protocols are properly deployed—encrypted, authenticated, hardened—they still retain native functionality that can be abused. Secure DNP3 still allows toggling of relays if the access control policy permits it. OPC UA can still allow full read/write access to critical variables if role configurations are lax. DDS Security prevents eavesdropping but not privilege misuse. Protocols cannot determine malicious intent. Secure communication ensures authenticity and confidentiality—but it does not enforce safe behavior.

In one red team engagement at a chemical processing plant, the defenders proudly declared their network was fully secured with OPC UA and TLS encryption. What they failed to mention —or perhaps didn't know—was that all access was granted through an anonymous user role with full control permissions. The red team accessed process variables, adjusted pump setpoints, and injected false alarms—all within fully encrypted, authenticated sessions. No alarms were triggered. No anomalies were detected. Security existed in form, not in function.

The deeper issue isn't the protocols. It's the environment they're dropped into. OT networks are not clean slates. They are battle-worn systems composed of long-lived devices, minimal firmware headroom, limited vendor support, and a deep-rooted fear of disruption. Protocol upgrades mean retesting, recertification, operator retraining, and compatibility checks. Each of these steps costs time and money. Each introduces risk. And when the alternative is to simply leave things alone—especially when the existing protocol "still works"— inertia wins. Even in organizations that want to modernize, procurement cycles and vendor constraints often prevent meaningful change. Security becomes an aspirational checkbox.

Secure protocols are not enough. They are necessary, but not sufficient. Without enforcement, without architectural support, without clear governance, they become decorative—technical symbols of risk reduction that do not actually reduce risk.

Security, at its best, is invisible—it protects without disrupting. But in industrial environments, security often becomes visible too late: during an audit, a red team exercise, or an incident. That's when the realization hits: the protocol was new, but the assumptions were old. The wire was different, but the trust was the same. And the adversary, once again, found a way in—not through a zero-day exploit, but through a deployment that was technically modern, yet operationally naïve.

If the next generation of industrial protocols is to succeed where their predecessors failed, it will require more than secure design. It will demand secure defaults. Opinionated configurations.

Clear guidance. Vendor enforcement. Auditable outcomes. And, perhaps most importantly, a cultural shift that treats protocol deployment as a security decision, not just an engineering one.

Because the language has changed, but the conversation remains exposed. And attackers, fluent in that language, are already listening.

CHAPTER 28 - CYBER-PHYSICAL CONVERGENCE AND SAFETY SYSTEMS

In the industrial world, safety systems serve as the final line of defense against catastrophe. Their role is not theoretical—they operate amid steel, pressure, chemicals, and heat, where consequences are measured not in data loss but in lives and environmental impact. Designed to function independently from digital systems, these mechanisms now face a new frontier: the encroachment of cyber threats into physical safety.

Cyber-physical systems—where digital control logic intersects with real-world physical processes—represent both a breakthrough and a liability. As control networks grow increasingly interconnected and software-driven, the once-clear boundary between cybersecurity and process safety begins to dissolve. This convergence now defines one of the most pressing and underexplored frontiers in industrial defense.

Historically, safety systems were designed to be standalone. They operated on independent logic solvers, often programmed through proprietary tools, and interfaced only minimally with broader control networks. Their purpose was binary: to trigger a shutdown, isolate a process, or vent pressure when predefined thresholds were crossed. These systems followed deterministic design principles: if X happens, do Y. They earned trust through simplicity and isolation. But over time, the demands for efficiency, centralized monitoring, and diagnostics introduced increased connectivity—and with it, new risks.

A critical vulnerability lies in how cybersecurity incidents can influence safety interlocks. In theory, safety systems operate independently. In practice, many now rely on networked data inputs or allow remote configuration—introducing paths for manipulation. An attacker need not override the final safety actuation; they can simply alter the criteria that determine whether that actuation occurs.

If a safety system receives manipulated data that falsely indicates normal operating conditions, it may not activate when it should. Conversely, if logic conditions are altered, the system may operate under a false sense of security even as physical thresholds are crossed. This shift redefines the threat: from forced shutdowns to silent failure of protective mechanisms.

The Stuxnet attack made this danger clear. At Iran's Natanz facility, the malware subtly altered the operating speeds of nuclear centrifuges while feeding false data to operators. The process was physically compromised, but the system screens displayed normal operations. This deception turned trusted instrumentation into an accomplice, illustrating how cyber attacks can simultaneously manipulate both the process and the perception of safety.

Generators are central to many safety systems, especially where uninterrupted power is critical for safe operations. Emergency diesel generators or turbine-based backups maintain power to safety instrumented systems, pressure relief devices, or cooling mechanisms. They are often the last defense during a grid failure. Yet these same systems, increasingly dependent on cyber control, present both a lifeline and a potential target.

The 2007 Aurora test by the U.S. Department of Homeland Security demonstrated how simple cyber manipulations could yield catastrophic physical outcomes. Researchers used a timed attack to open and close a generator's circuit breakers out of sync with the grid. The result was destructive torque that tore through the generator's internals. No malware was required—just precise control over the timing interface. The implications were stark: cyber attackers could destroy critical equipment using nothing more than trusted interfaces and physics.

These risks bring into focus two foundational safety philosophies: fail-safe and fail-operational. Fail-safe systems default to a secure state—typically by shutting down—during a fault. Fail-operational systems, in contrast, aim to sustain operation despite failures. Choosing between them is not merely technical; it's strategic. The cybersecurity implication is that fail-safe systems may resist certain cyber threats more robustly—but only if the system can correctly detect unsafe conditions in the first place.

A malicious actor who delays actuation by milliseconds or falsifies safety status can still provoke catastrophic outcomes. Inversely, a malicious shutdown may be used as a weapon itself—triggering economic damage, pressure surges, or triggering downstream instability. Safety decisions, therefore, must balance both the risk of failure and the risk of false activation.

To mitigate these risks, industrial safety designs adopt Safety Integrity Levels (SILs), metrics defined in standards like IEC 61508 and 61511. SILs quantify the probability of failure on demand, ranging from SIL 1 to SIL 4, each step representing an order-of-magnitude increase in reliability. SIL 3 or 4 systems are typically required in high-risk industries like nuclear, petrochemical, and aviation.

Achieving a target SIL level requires comprehensive hazard and risk assessments, using methodologies like HAZOP and LOPA. These feed into the design of safety instrumented functions (SIFs), which must be implemented with precise hardware, software, and procedural controls. Yet, the origin of SIL was reliability—not adversarial manipulation. Its assumptions often break down in the presence of deliberate sabotage.

A highly reliable but easily manipulated safety system is not safe. Therefore, cybersecurity principles must now overlay functional safety design. Logic solvers should be hardened, engineering workstations secured, and safety configurations validated continuously. It is not enough for inputs to be accurate —their integrity must be proven.

Defense-in-depth must extend beyond operational networks and into the heart of safety architecture. Segmentation is only effective if communications are strictly controlled—ideally enforced through hardware boundaries such as data diodes. Engineering workstations should be isolated, access tightly audited, and safety logic cryptographically signed to prevent unauthorized changes. These are not aspirational controls— they are essential in a world where safety systems are deliberate targets.

Redundancy and diversification also define resilient safety design. Redundancy ensures that a single point of failure —accidental or malicious—cannot disable protection. But identical systems are identically vulnerable. Diversification— across vendors, operating systems, and control paths—makes successful exploitation significantly harder, especially for targeted attacks.

This need for architectural resilience became alarmingly real with the Triton/Trisis attack. At a Saudi petrochemical plant in 2017, custom malware targeted a Schneider Electric Triconex SIS, attempting to reprogram its logic and disable protective functions. The goal was not immediate disruption, but to quietly remove safeguards. The attack was discovered only after a misstep triggered a shutdown. Triton shattered the illusion that safety systems were immune.

It showed that availability is not integrity. A safety system online but compromised is far more dangerous than one that has failed safely. The attack emphasized the need for segmentation, patching, logging, and strict access control in safety-critical environments.

Awareness of the cyber-physical nexus has grown, but challenges persist. Many facilities still operate under assumptions of air gaps or obscurity. Others lack the resources to modernize legacy systems or the organizational cohesion to bring IT and OT into alignment. Inertia—not just exposure—is the threat. Cybersecurity must now be seen as intrinsic to safety.

This shift requires education, funding, and leadership. Safety engineers must understand cyber threats; security professionals must respect process control realities. Neither can succeed alone. Together, they must build frameworks that address deliberate compromise, not just random failure.

Forward-looking organizations now assess safety and cybersecurity together. Design reviews test not only hardware reliability but resistance to logic corruption. They verify safety functions against tampering and include forensic capabilities in system design. They recognize that survivability under attack is now as critical as uptime.

This convergence is not just technical—it is cultural. It demands new thinking about trust, verification, and cross-discipline collaboration. The control room and SOC are no longer separate. They are partners in a shared mission to safeguard human life and industrial continuity.

This chapter is not a conclusion but a beginning. As systems grow more connected and threats more adaptive, the convergence of safety and cybersecurity must be embedded in every layer of design, operation, and mindset. Separation is no longer protection. It is vulnerability. Our challenge is not only to prevent failure, but to detect and resist compromise that hides in plain sight.

CHAPTER 29 – WHEN SENSORS LIE: FIELD DEVICE INTEGRITY AND PHYSICAL SIGNAL TAMPERING

Trust in industrial environments begins with measurement. The values that appear on a control panel, trend in a historian, or trigger an interlock are all derived from a set of physical inputs—temperatures, pressures, flows, levels, voltages. These values originate not from software but from transducers and field instruments mounted to pipes, tanks, and wires. In OT environments, these sensors are often considered neutral, objective, and inherently truthful. But in adversarial settings, that assumption is deeply flawed. Sensors can lie. And when they do, the systems that rely on them can be made to fail not because they were attacked directly, but because they believed something that wasn't real.

At the center of this risk is the fundamental reality that sensors translate the physical world into digital signals. Thermocouples generate voltages. RTDs change resistance. Flowmeters pulse. Transmitters modulate analog signals, often in 4–20 mA current loops, before converting those values into registers or packets. That translation process creates surface area—not just for noise or failure, but for manipulation. A device that receives data from a field sensor is not reading the process itself; it's reading an interpretation of that process. And interpretations can be manipulated.

The most direct way sensors are attacked is through spoofing—feeding them values that appear valid but do not reflect actual conditions. A temperature sensor mounted to a process pipe can be cooled or heated artificially. A pressure transducer can be pulsed with compressed air. An ultrasonic level sensor can be misled with audio interference or placed at an angle that distorts reflection. In environments where signal conditioning is minimal or absent, even low-effort attacks can generate false readings. And when those readings drive logic decisions—start a pump, close a valve, trigger a trip—false inputs lead to real outcomes.

More subtle is the manipulation of signals within the device. Many modern sensors are not passive—they include firmware, ADCs, calibration routines, and diagnostics. In some architectures, they are networked directly, reporting via HART, Foundation Fieldbus, or Ethernet-based protocols. If the firmware inside that device is compromised, it can continue to report "normal" values even as the process deviates wildly. In security parlance, this is not denial of service—it is denial of integrity. The data channel remains open. The system believes it is safe. But it has been blinded.

This model was demonstrated most famously in the Stuxnet attack, where not only PLC logic was altered, but sensor values were intercepted and spoofed. Centrifuge speeds were pushed to unsafe levels while the operators observed perfectly normal values on their control screens. The feedback loop was poisoned. The attackers didn't just send bad commands—they suppressed evidence of those commands by feeding the system back its own expectations. That kind of manipulation is powerful not because it breaks things, but because it allows them to continue breaking undetected.

The 2017 Triton/Trisis attack also exploited trust in sensor data. While its payload targeted SIS logic controllers, its success relied on crafting conditions where sensor input was manipulated—or at least misrepresented—to delay or disable trip logic. The safety systems trusted what they were told, not what was actually happening. That trust, exploited carefully, allowed the attacker to approach the edge of catastrophic failure without sounding alarms.

Sensor manipulation doesn't require a zero-day or exotic toolkit. Off-the-shelf oscilloscopes, loop simulators, and signal injectors are enough to create plausible inputs. In red team engagements, attackers have used 4–20 mA simulators to fool temperature and flow sensors, triggering alarms or suppressing them altogether. One engineer discovered a wireless HART pressure sensor that could be reconfigured using a default PIN over Bluetooth. With a few commands, the device's pressure range was shifted upward, making dangerously high values appear normal. No passwords were bypassed. The system responded exactly as it was designed to.

The risk is not only physical. Firmware within sensor devices is rarely scrutinized during procurement or commissioning. Yet attackers targeting the supply chain could embed logic to delay alarms, introduce subtle drift, or transmit normal values even when the hardware senses abnormality. In many cases, calibration tables and conversion factors are stored in modifiable flash memory. A compromised or altered firmware update—whether from a vendor, integrator, or malicious third party—can silently rewire how the device interprets the world. And because most industrial sensors are closed systems with no outbound authentication, the process logic simply accepts what it's given.

Compounding this are the insecure protocols through which sensors communicate. The HART protocol, still widely used, allows configuration and diagnostics to travel over the same analog loop as the signal, often with no encryption or authentication. Foundation Fieldbus sensors often expose block-level control that can be reprogrammed if access is granted—sometimes by default. Modbus-based sensors, especially those embedded in legacy RTUs, may expose entire configuration maps to unauthenticated writes, enabling remote attackers to redefine what "normal" even looks like.

Sensor spoofing isn't always technical. Environmental deception is becoming increasingly viable as attackers and red teams recognize how easily physical signals can be distorted. Heating a thermal sensor with a directional heat gun, redirecting ultrasonic signals with reflective plates, or dampening capacitive touch sensors with shielding foil can all alter behavior. Radio frequency interference can induce false readings in analog sensors. In one field exercise, a team used a small transmitter to introduce EMI across an unshielded sensor line, causing a flowmeter to spike erratically. No data packets were forged. The sensor simply reported what it "saw."

Even when sensors aren't deceived, humans are. Control room operators are trained to trust their interfaces, not question them. If the HMI shows a valve is closed and the flow is zero, it's assumed to be true—even if a noise in the background suggests otherwise. This bias toward digital truth is exploitable. In one incident, a tank level sensor failed silently and was overridden by an operator, based on a persistent false reading. The tank overflowed within minutes. The incident report blamed operator error. No one asked if the sensor had lied first.

More dangerous still are situations where false data leads to incorrect overrides of safety systems. In industries like oil and gas, chemical processing, and energy generation, sensors trigger interlocks and trips designed to prevent catastrophic outcomes. If a manipulated sensor prevents that trigger—either through suppression or delay—the system becomes unsafe by design. And because the sensor "said everything was fine," root cause analysis often points away from compromise.

Redundancy is not always a cure. Triplicated sensors with majority voting logic are vulnerable to coordinated spoofing or environmental factors that affect all three at once. Attackers can manipulate timing, delay one input slightly, or skew values just enough to create chaos in logic comparisons. In tightly packed equipment racks, a single physical manipulation—like a directed heat source—can affect multiple sensors. When redundancy fails, it fails with confidence.

And beyond failure, there's drift. In one documented case, attackers slowly manipulated calibration tables over weeks, shifting a pressure sensor's zero point so subtly that operators compensated without realizing it. The system didn't break—it degraded. Valves wore out faster. Compressors operated outside design margins. But nothing tripped. No alerts fired. The plant limped along, burdened by a lie that looked like truth.

This type of attack can be catastrophic not only for the process but for compliance. In regulated sectors like pharmaceuticals, nuclear energy, and aviation, false sensor data can lead to unreported violations. Batch integrity, safety certification, and emission thresholds are based on assumed measurement accuracy. If that accuracy is compromised—intentionally or not—entire audit trails collapse. Safety Integrity Level (SIL) calculations assume defined error models. Sensor spoofing nullifies those models. A plant may be operating out of bounds, legally and physically, without ever realizing it.

Detection of sensor lies requires more than anomaly detection. It demands system-level thinking. Pump speed, pressure, and flow should be correlated. Energy input and thermal response should match. Control actions should yield expected sensor feedback within known timing windows. When these patterns deviate, there may be more at play than faulty equipment. There may be a lie.

Advanced environments use digital twins to simulate process expectations and compare them against real-time data. These models can detect divergences, but they require clean, trusted data to function. Others use active sensing—sending known pulses into the system and verifying the response—to catch spoofing or sensor lag. But most facilities aren't ready for such sophistication. What they can do is baseline behavior, test response timing, and verify process congruence across systems.

And most critically, they can stop assuming that sensors are passive, dumb, and trustworthy. They are intelligent endpoints with memory, interfaces, and logic. They are programmable. They are updatable. And they are vulnerable.

The assumption that sensors are truthful is embedded deeply in both control logic and human trust. Operators will often believe what the system shows them, even when physical reality disagrees. If the screen says the tank is full, they may ignore the sound of it running dry. If the graph shows the valve is closed, they may not notice the pressure dropping. This human dependency on digital readout creates a vulnerability in perception—one that skilled attackers can exploit.

Because when a sensor lies, it doesn't just confuse the system. It confuses the people who rely on it. And once trust in measurement is broken, the entire architecture of industrial control begins to unravel.

CHAPTER 30 –
THE FAKE PUMP IS
LISTENING: DECEPTION,
HONEYPOTS, AND
DEFENSIVE ILLUSIONS

Most cybersecurity defenses are reactive. They wait to detect, log, or block something malicious—after it has already touched the system. Firewalls enforce policies. Endpoint protection flags signatures. Network detection systems raise alerts. But what happens when defenders shift from passively detecting to actively deceiving? What happens when the attacker's target turns out to be bait?

This is the premise behind deception technologies, decoy systems, and industrial honeypots—tools that don't simply monitor the environment, but manipulate the adversary's perception of it. In high-stakes OT environments, where intrusion often precedes damage, deception offers an alternative posture: instead of just defending the crown jewels, defenders can *invite* attackers to interact with fakes. And while attackers talk to the fake pump, the real system listens.

The idea of deploying decoys in OT is not new, but it's gaining urgency. Traditional visibility tools—packet capture, log analysis, anomaly detection—are limited by architecture and access. Many legacy devices offer no telemetry. Deep packet inspection may be blocked by proprietary protocols or encrypted tunnels. And in segmented environments, defenders often lack continuous insight into lateral movement within the OT enclave. This leaves critical gaps. Deception fills them—not by sealing off the gaps, but by making them ambiguous. If attackers cannot trust the environment they see, they are forced to hesitate, second-guess, or reveal their tactics.

The roots of honeypot technology lie in early IT history. Tools like *BackOfficer Friendly*, *Deception Toolkit*, and later *Honeyd* introduced the idea of listening, logging, and misleading. Over time, these evolved into honeynets—entire fake networks built to observe attacker behavior. The Honeynet Project pioneered much of this work, and in the 2010s, OT-specific honeypots began to appear: *Conpot*, *GasPot*, *GridPot*, and *HoneyPLC* offered industrialized decoys with support for Modbus, DNP3, BACnet, and S7Comm. These efforts translated deception into the physical domain—offering a bridge between network surveillance and process-layer defense.

Industrial honeypots now come in several forms. Some are full-stack emulations—software that mimics PLCs, RTUs, or control panels at the protocol level. Others are low-interaction decoys, emulating only ports and banner responses. High-fidelity deception platforms simulate entire control networks, complete with HMI screens, register maps, and logic behavior. In one configuration, a "ghost" water treatment plant was built inside a real utility network—unreachable from the outside but visible to any attacker who breached the perimeter. The goal wasn't just to observe; it was to confuse.

The most effective decoys are indistinguishable from their real counterparts. They use identical firmware versions, mirror real naming conventions, and mimic traffic patterns down to timing, payload size, and error behavior. In some cases, real devices are cloned, with their communications copied and replayed to produce plausible background chatter. This authenticity is key. If the attacker suspects the device is fake, the deception fails. But if they believe it's a real pressure sensor or valve controller, they may engage—probing, scanning, or issuing commands that would otherwise remain hidden.

That engagement is where the value lies. Every interaction with a honeypot reveals intent. Attackers who enumerate registers, attempt writes, or scan known service ports aren't innocent explorers—they're looking for leverage. A honeypot captures those signals. It records command syntax, timing patterns, and fingerprinting techniques. In some platforms, it even logs keystrokes, extracts attacker tooling, or executes payloads in a controlled sandbox. The result is an intelligence feed—not just an alert. Analysts can correlate behavior, trace infrastructure, and understand adversary capability long before the real system is touched.

In real-world incidents, deception has exposed attacks that bypassed traditional defenses. In one case, a contractor's laptop was compromised while off-site. When the attacker reconnected to the OT environment through a trusted tunnel, they landed in a decoy segment populated with fake PLCs. Believing the network was legitimate, they ran scripts to pull memory, scan for broadcast responses, and issue writes to command points. None of it reached the live systems. But it gave defenders a play-by-play of the intrusion—complete with attacker IPs, payloads, and timing. That intelligence hardened the real environment before the attacker even tried again.

Deception also buys time. In environments where response windows are measured in seconds, early detection is critical. A write attempt to a honeypot is not a delayed alert—it's an immediate signal of unauthorized behavior. Unlike anomaly detection systems that require baselining or machine learning models that generate false positives, honeypots don't guess. They operate on the principle of *impossibility*. If no legitimate user should interact with the fake pump, any interaction is malicious. This clarity reduces cognitive load, speeds triage, and enables decisive response.

But deception doesn't live in a vacuum. It becomes

exponentially more powerful when integrated into broader detection infrastructure. Honeypot signals should feed into SIEM and SOAR platforms, where they can trigger automated correlation with endpoint telemetry, firewall logs, or intrusion alerts. Deception events can enrich threat hunting and incident response, linking attacker behavior to timeframes and lateral movement. Some organizations integrate honeypots directly with OT-aware NIDS platforms—cross-validating traffic captured on decoy interfaces with that seen elsewhere. A honeypot, well placed, becomes a high-fidelity sensor—not just a tripwire.

Still, there are technical challenges that require care. Faking an OT device is not like emulating a web server. Industrial protocols are timing-sensitive, stateful, and often proprietary. Modbus devices respond with precise delays. DNP3 devices maintain unsolicited message intervals. S7Comm and CIP devices expose quirks in packet sequencing and object identifiers. If a decoy doesn't behave naturally—if its register map is too sparse, if its error codes are generic, or if it fails to respond to unexpected commands—an experienced adversary may detect the deception. High-fidelity requires high accuracy.

Deception also reveals its value against internal threats. While many honeypot discussions focus on nation-state actors or ransomware groups, insider threats are often more subtle and persistent. A contractor who accesses unauthorized areas of the network, a technician who experiments with undocumented commands, or a disgruntled employee scanning devices late at night—all can be detected if they probe a decoy. Honeypots aren't just about stopping attackers. They're about detecting behavior that breaks policy, even before it breaks the system.

This makes deception valuable in third-party and vendor monitoring as well. If a vendor's cloud-connected device or management tunnel starts reaching out to unexpected subnets —or interacting with decoy devices—an alert can be raised. A honeypot can detect the compromise of an otherwise trusted supply chain partner, catching signals that would never show up in traditional endpoint or perimeter defenses. It's a form of outbound validation. If a trusted asset talks to a known fake, something's gone wrong.

But deception is not a silver bullet. Deploying it incorrectly can create risk. Low-fidelity honeypots may generate false positives. Poorly placed decoys may overload SOC teams with noise. Overzealous deployment can clash with operational and audit concerns. And in tightly regulated ICS environments, even non-functional systems must often go through rigorous change management or vendor certification. Adding a honeypot isn't always politically or procedurally simple. It requires planning, documentation, and buy-in.

There are philosophical objections as well. Some organizations view honeypots as borderline entrapment, or worry about legal exposure when attackers are "lured" into interacting with them. Others resist the idea of operationalizing deception—worried that it may be seen as a gimmick, or may draw attention away from more fundamental security improvements. These concerns aren't baseless. Deception must be purposeful. It must be tested, maintained, and reviewed regularly. If not, it becomes just another sensor collecting dust.

Despite this, many organizations are embracing deception as a strategic layer. Some build their own—Python scripts that emulate PLCs, virtualized honeynets mapped to unused IP ranges, or raspberry pi decoys dropped into flat networks. Others adopt commercial deception platforms that integrate into their security stack. The most advanced defenders use deception not only for attacker detection, but for validation of their own detection. Red teams are challenged to avoid the decoys. Blue teams are measured on how quickly they respond when the fake pump gets touched.

One powerful example emerged from a fusion energy facility where researchers deployed a decoy control console on a test network. When an attacker gained access through a vulnerable printer server, they found what appeared to be a live operations panel. They issued benign queries. Then they issued write commands. Then they attempted to push firmware. Every action was mirrored in a containment layer—safe, logged, and replayed to investigators. The real systems were untouched. But the defense team now had a blueprint of how the adversary thought.

The value of deception is not in how it protects. It's in how it reveals. It transforms passive defense into interactive intelligence. It slows adversaries, sows doubt, and exposes tradecraft. In industrial environments—where attackers may dwell quietly, explore slowly, and strike only once—deception may be the only signal available.

Because sometimes, the only way to catch someone watching is to let them see something worth attacking—and make sure it's fake.

CHAPTER 31 – MIRRORED WORLDS: DIGITAL TWINS, SIMULATION, AND THE ILLUSION OF CONTROL

There was a time when the only way to understand how a machine worked was to watch it move. Pumps had to be inspected. Pipes had to be traced. Temperatures had to be taken with physical instruments. The system revealed itself through vibration, sound, and flow. But now, increasingly, systems are understood not by looking at the equipment, but by watching its reflection—a digital twin, rendered in dashboards and 3D views, glowing on an HMI or piped into a cloud. This mirror offers visibility, precision, and real-time insight. But it also introduces something more subtle. It introduces the risk that operators, engineers, and even security teams will confuse the model with the thing it represents.

Digital twins are not simply visualizations. They are synchronized models of real-world systems—fed by sensors, enriched by logic, and in many cases, bi-directional. They simulate process states, track wear, model environmental impact, and enable predictive maintenance. In theory, a digital twin allows you to understand what's happening, what might happen next, and what would happen if you intervened. The promise is elegant: complete visibility, constant feedback, and the power to experiment safely.

In industrial settings, the digital twin can span an entire operation—from the geometry of a turbine blade to the thermal profile of a power plant. These models are built from CAD files, physics-based simulators, historical telemetry, and real-time operational data. They are refined over time as new inputs arrive. Eventually, they behave convincingly. The mirrored world becomes responsive. You adjust a setting, and the model reflects the outcome. You simulate a fault, and the twin predicts what would occur. It becomes a sandbox—a synthetic twin of the real system.

But beneath this elegance lies a problem as old as computing itself: the model is never the system. It is a representation. And when that representation is incomplete, misaligned, or out of sync, decisions made in the mirrored world can have catastrophic consequences in the physical one.

Many organizations mistakenly use the term "digital twin" to describe any animated dashboard or HMI screen. But true digital twins go beyond visualization—they incorporate real physics, simulation, and predictive feedback. They react, adapt, and even anticipate. A mimic is not a twin. A screen showing tank levels is not the same as a model that simulates their behavior under stress. This distinction matters, because the deeper the reliance on that model, the more dangerous it becomes when misunderstood.

In some cases, the twin is treated as the source of truth. Operators consult the digital model to understand tank levels, flow rates, or chemical composition. But if the inputs are corrupted—whether by failure, miscalibration, or manipulation—the model reflects a fiction. In security terms, this is not a failure of the model. It is a failure of trust. And the more operators trust the twin, the less they scrutinize reality. This isn't just an operational risk—it's a psychological one.

Digital twins create a veneer of control, a belief that because we can simulate, we understand. But simulation is always a function of assumptions. It requires initial conditions, governing rules, and boundaries. If those boundaries are exceeded—if the system behaves in a way not anticipated by the model—then the twin may not just be wrong, it may be dangerously misleading. In one incident at a high-volume packaging plant, the twin continued to show normal conveyor speed and alignment, even as a mechanical fault introduced a growing deviation. The sensors were feeding old data. The model believed it. And the operators, trusting the model, failed to see the problem until the system jammed catastrophically.

In another case, a logistics facility used a digital twin to manage automated fulfillment lanes. When a firmware patch added slight delays in actuator timing, the twin's model—which hadn't been updated—failed to account for the latency. A change in buffer logic, made based on simulated clearance times, caused real-world pallet collisions. The simulation was clean. The execution was chaos.

From a cybersecurity standpoint, attackers have begun exploring how to manipulate twins—not just to spoof operators, but to delay detection. By falsifying sensor inputs, adversaries can keep the twin in sync with their narrative, even as the real system deviates. In one red team scenario, attackers injected falsified flow rates into a chemical processing twin, convincing the control system that feedstocks were balanced. In reality, a critical ratio was falling out of spec. The model validated the lie, and the interlocks never tripped.

Some digital twins include replay and historical simulation tools that allow forward projection or condition-based maintenance modeling. These are powerful features—but if the historical record is manipulated, the projections become poisoned. A subtle falsification of runtime hours or temperature profiles can convince a maintenance system to delay service or falsely approve operation. The attack occurs in the model, but the consequence unfolds in steel and steam.

Digital twins also inherit the attack surfaces of their integrations. Twins that rely on cloud telemetry, API access to OT systems, or synchronization with vendor analytics platforms open new paths. A twin with read/write access into control systems is effectively another control node. If compromised, it may issue dangerous commands without raising suspicion—because it looks like optimization. Some vendors even bundle twins into IoT platforms that come with hardcoded credentials, shared cloud brokers, and always-on update paths. In some environments, the twin isn't just a mirror —it's a conduit.

There is also the question of provenance. Where did the data feeding the twin come from? How was it collected, and how often? Was it signed? Was it validated? Many twins operate on data that passes through multiple processing layers—edge nodes, gateways, data historians, API translation layers—each of which can be silently tampered with. A sophisticated attacker doesn't need to attack the twin or the machine. They can intercept the stream between them.

Beyond technology, digital twins are reshaping the culture of operations. As teams grow dependent on the twin, their ability to interpret raw system behavior—noise, vibration, heat, tension—fades. Junior operators may be trained entirely on the twin and never learn the physical instincts their predecessors relied on. In one facility, a simulated valve profile was trusted over the sound of a real valve hammering against its seat. The result was a catastrophic seal failure that no model could predict —but a veteran could have heard.

Digital twins are also increasingly promoted as cyber-resilient tools. Vendors claim their twins can model ransomware attacks, simulate failover scenarios, or help assess recovery timelines. But these models are typically built on clean, idealized assumptions. They do not simulate partial connectivity, insider misuse, misconfigured air gaps, or decades of undocumented patches. They model best-case chaos—not real chaos. There is danger in treating them as planning tools without hard validation.

Digital twins are often created with a specific purpose—design testing, equipment commissioning, or predictive maintenance modeling—but then repurposed for runtime operations without any formal revalidation. A twin that was accurate during a greenfield deployment may no longer match the physical plant after ten firmware updates, three sensor replacements, and one undocumented retrofit. Yet the model persists, and operators continue to rely on it as if it were truth. The assumptions baked into the twin become invisible—until the moment they're violated.

This repurposing problem is compounded by fragmented ownership. In many organizations, digital twins are touched by IT teams who manage infrastructure, OT teams who run the physical process, and vendors who own the simulation engine itself. None of these parties may have full visibility into how the twin is being used or updated. A vendor may push a model update unaware of plant-floor changes. An IT team may back up and restore a twin without verifying its synchronization. When no one owns the full picture, the twin becomes a shared risk with no single steward.

In post-incident scenarios, digital twins introduce yet another layer of complexity. Some twins are designed to keep simulating even when the physical system goes offline—creating a misleading sense of continuity. Others are consulted during disaster recovery as if they were canonical logs of operational history. But if the twin's inputs were falsified—or if the twin itself was modified—then its historical record cannot be trusted. An attacker who compromises a twin may not just affect real-time operations but rewrite the forensic trail.

Indeed, if attackers gain access to the twin, the risks are even greater. Unlike traditional SCADA systems that might offer limited visibility, a well-built twin often provides full topology, process logic, and performance data. An adversary who can study the twin can learn pressure thresholds, flow tolerances, and even safety interlock behavior—all without ever touching the actual system. In this way, the twin becomes a blueprint for targeted sabotage. It offers not just a map, but a simulation environment where attackers can test ideas in safety.

Interoperability is another misunderstood promise. Vendors often market their twins as universally integratable, capable of linking with other models, enterprise platforms, or simulation environments. In practice, these integrations depend on shared ontologies, synchronized data schemas, and precise mappings of physical reality. When one link in that chain shifts— a renamed asset, a changed control tag, a modified fieldbus configuration—the integration may silently break. Worse, the systems may continue exchanging data without realizing they're misaligned. The illusion of harmony becomes a silent divergence.

None of this is to say digital twins should be rejected. But they must be treated as mirrors—not oracles. They require validation. They must be tested against real-world behavior. They should be run with adversarial inputs and fuzzed against corner cases. They must be air-gapped from decision-making logic unless explicitly authorized. And above all, they must be understood.

The model is not the machine. And the moment we forget that, we stop watching the process and begin watching its shadow.

CHAPTER 32 – LIVE FIRE IN A LIVE PLANT: RED AND BLUE TEAMS IN CYBER-PHYSICAL EXERCISES

It begins with a compromise. Not the breach—yet—but the compromise between engineering and cybersecurity, between safety and simulation, between those who build and those who probe. A red team wants realism. A blue team wants insight. The operators want predictability. Management wants assurance. And threading between all of them is the quiet, persistent fear: what happens when the simulation isn't synthetic enough?

This is what makes live fire different. It's not a tabletop exercise. It's not packet captures and PowerPoint. It's not a twin model glowing in a clean cloud console. It's a real controller running real logic driving real machinery, and the people standing next to it are betting that the test won't break the process they depend on. Live fire in a live plant isn't just about testing defenses. It's about testing coordination. And trust. And judgment.

The plant had agreed—reluctantly—to host a joint red-blue exercise. It was a mid-sized refining facility, with a mix of legacy controllers, Windows-based HMI systems, and a few recent upgrades tied into a cloud analytics platform. The process wasn't high hazard, but it wasn't low either. Mistakes had consequences: misaligned flows, overpressured tanks, cross-contaminated batches. Production couldn't be stopped, so the test had to be staged while live units were running. It would be a narrow slice of a wider engagement—a focused scenario targeting the most common failure modes identified in past incidents: protocol abuse, misused trust, credential leakage, and operator disorientation.

The red team began in familiar territory—network reconnaissance, asset enumeration, and interface mapping. But this time, there were boundaries: no denial-of-service, no direct writes to live logic unless approved in real-time, and no persistent backdoors. This wasn't a capture-the-flag. It was a joint learning environment. The red team wasn't there to win. They were there to reveal.

The blue team wasn't just security analysts. It was operations, shift leads, instrumentation techs, control room supervisors. For once, the model of defense included the people who would live through the aftermath of an attack. And that changed the tone completely. The defenders weren't watching alerts. They were watching pressures. Watching people. Watching for signs that something subtle had gone wrong—before it became obvious.

Phase one was credential testing. The red team compromised a shared engineering laptop that hadn't rotated passwords since commissioning. It had saved sessions for two remote gateways —one for a historian, the other for a process control terminal inside a Level 2 VLAN. The attack was silent. No malware, no persistence. Just logging in through a VPN the team had forgotten was still enabled.

The blue team caught it—but not through firewalls. One of the operators noticed that the terminal lights flickered. Briefly. Just long enough to prompt him to ask why the historian had queried the PLC twice in a row. That question led to a review of historian logs, which led to an alert, which led to a cross-team meeting before the red team had even pivoted. It wasn't technology that won the first round. It was attention.

Phase two simulated command injection. This time, the red team mimicked a protocol-level replay attack. They captured legitimate Modbus traffic from a field device using a tap on a mirrored port, replayed it back during an operator shift change, and timed it to align with a known sensor warmup cycle. The goal was subtle: alter a pump start time by 30 seconds and see if anyone noticed.

They didn't. The command was accepted. The delay caused a flow imbalance. A downstream tank level dropped just slightly below expected, which caused a technician to manually adjust the inflow rate—not because he thought it was under attack, but because he believed it was a process deviation. In doing so, he unknowingly reinforced the attacker's illusion.

But here's where live fire changes everything.

Because when the blue team analyzed the HMI logs afterward, they saw the deviation. They saw the replay pattern. And they realized something: they would never have caught that in a passive monitoring system. It was only because the shift tech annotated the deviation manually—writing down the pressure adjustment on his worksheet—that the anomaly was correlated. People filled in the gaps that machines missed. The red team had succeeded in deception. But the blue team succeeded in contextual memory.

Phase three was the real test. The red team was allowed to simulate a partial takeover of an engineering workstation using a mock payload delivered through a phished spreadsheet —pre-arranged, sandboxed, and with signed-off execution. The goal wasn't compromise. The goal was confusion. The malware launched a cloned HMI interface that looked identical to the real one. But it silently suppressed a single alarm: a low-level warning on a feedstock tank used to buffer transitions during changeovers.

The cloned HMI ran for nearly an hour.

Operators noticed that it looked... clean. Too clean. No small alerts. No transient errors. No intermittent warnings about IO errors from the backup level sensor. One of them reached under the console, pulled out a diagnostic handheld, and plugged it into the fieldbus segment.

That moment changed the test.

Because it wasn't in the playbook. It wasn't part of the response plan. It was a habit. A behavior learned through years of not trusting the screens. And it revealed that the tank was almost empty. If the system had continued without correction, the next batch would have pulled air into the main feed, destabilizing the product mixture and contaminating thousands of gallons of processed material. The red team had created the perfect silent fault. And the blue team had caught it through instinct.

What the simulation proved wasn't that the red team could get in. Everyone already knew that. What it proved was that real detection lives in the convergence zone—where human expertise, behavioral nuance, and slight irregularities intersect. The best SOC in the world wouldn't have caught what that technician saw in a flicker of interface perfection.

In the post-exercise review, both teams sat together for the first time. The red team walked through their payloads, their network captures, their access chains. The blue team walked through what they felt. What they saw. What made them stop and ask: why is this off? One by one, a pattern emerged. Every moment of successful defense had come from the lived experience of operators. From a tech who knew when valves usually hissed. From a lead who knew that no system ever ran that clean. From a line worker who knew that every shift begins with a warning or two—so when there were none, something was wrong.

It wasn't about technology. It was about texture.

That lesson reshaped how both teams thought about defense. The red team began modeling not just network paths, but cognitive load—understanding what a real operator expects to see and what they'll ignore. They learned that perfect silence is often the loudest indicator of compromise in an environment where something is always broken. And the blue team stopped waiting for alerts to tell them what was wrong. They began trusting their intuition again.

More importantly, leadership saw the value of full-spectrum simulation. The company didn't just invest in new monitoring tools—they invested in cross-training. Security staff spent days on the line learning how process flow actually behaved. Engineers were briefed on attack anatomy and asked to help model consequence, not just vulnerability. The firewall rules were updated. The twin model was decoupled from live inputs during drills. And operators were given one new power: the right to halt a test if something didn't feel right.

Because in a live plant, the most important signal may not be in the packet or the payload. It may be in a glance. A hesitation. A scribbled note in a margin. A technician standing a little too long at a screen that looks too perfect.

Live fire in a live plant is not about breaking systems. It's about learning where they already bend. And when red and blue teams meet not as adversaries, but as mirrors, they stop proving risk—and start mapping reality.

PART V
Governance, Risk, and the Future of Industrial Protocols

CHAPTER 33 – PAPER SHIELDS: COMPLIANCE, REGULATION, AND THE ILLUSION OF SECURITY

On paper, everything was perfect. The diagrams were up to date. The firewall rules were documented. The passwords were rotated. The audit logs were stored. The training had been completed. The risk register had no red flags, and the report to executive leadership closed with a confident statement: "We are compliant."

And yet, when the incident happened, none of that mattered.

The breach didn't come through an unpatched vulnerability or a sophisticated zero-day. It came through a trusted connection, a vendor maintenance tunnel, and a credential that no one had remembered to revoke. The intrusion wasn't detected by the SIEM. It wasn't stopped by the firewall. It wasn't escalated because, technically, it didn't violate policy. It flowed neatly within the lanes defined by compliance—and landed squarely inside the heart of the process control environment.

This is the dangerous illusion: that if you do what the regulations require, you have done enough.

In industrial cybersecurity, compliance is often treated as a synonym for security. Audits are passed. Controls are mapped. Policies are reviewed. But security is not an exercise in documentation. It is not the presence of controls—it is the absence of consequence. And in too many cases, the paperwork is pristine while the infrastructure it describes is riddled with fragility.

Regulations like NERC-CIP, NEI 08-09, ISA/IEC 62443, and NIST 800-53 are critical frameworks. They establish baseline expectations, define categories of risk, and formalize language around roles, responsibilities, and protections. They are necessary. But they are not sufficient. Because the moment compliance becomes the *goal* rather than a *byproduct* of doing security right, the result is a defensive architecture that looks complete in a binder but breaks the moment an adversary deviates from the script.

Paper shields are seductive because they give the illusion of control. They allow a plant manager to say, "We're covered." They allow an executive to brief the board with confidence. They allow regulators to check the box and move on. But paper doesn't block packets. Paper doesn't stop rogue scripts. Paper doesn't recognize that the firewall was misconfigured after the last network change. Paper doesn't ask what changed in the field. It only asks whether the documentation reflects what *should* be.

In one facility, a compliance audit showed perfect segmentation between corporate and OT networks. VLANs were defined. Firewalls were documented. ACLs were signed off. But a temporary connection had been left open between two engineering subnets during a PLC firmware update—weeks before the audit. It was never removed. No one noticed. And the documentation didn't mention it, because the documentation reflected policy, not reality. The path existed, and an attacker used it. The paperwork was never touched.

In another case, a risk register listed third-party access as a "monitored control" with "low residual risk." The justification? All vendors were required to use jump hosts with two-factor authentication. But in practice, a subset of legacy connections bypassed the jump host entirely—because older systems couldn't authenticate through it. The exception was documented. The mitigation was noted. But the control failed the moment a vendor's laptop was compromised off-site. The attacker used the old tunnel. The risk register stayed green until it turned black.

These stories are not anomalies. They are patterns.

The problem is not the frameworks. The problem is the substitution of *conformance* for *effectiveness*. A control is not secure just because it is documented. A process is not resilient just because it has been signed off. And a system is not defended just because the checklist has been completed. In OT, defenses must *work under pressure*, not just exist on paper.

Compliance often shapes security behavior—not because it reflects the most urgent threats, but because it drives budgeting, accountability, and visibility. In many organizations, cybersecurity funding is tied directly to audit requirements. Teams are incentivized to complete control mappings and maintain documentation more than to test real-world resilience. This shifts the focus from actual defense to audit performance. Projects that don't explicitly map to a regulatory requirement are deprioritized or shelved entirely—even if they close known operational risks.

This is compounded by regulatory lag. Frameworks are often years behind emerging threat realities. Many compliance programs were written in the era of insider threats and commodity malware—not persistent, nation-state-backed supply chain attacks. Password rotation schedules, unidirectional firewall assumptions, and logging retention requirements often fail to account for the dwell time and tactics of modern adversaries. A system can meet every compliance objective and still be wildly unprepared for the adversaries who know how to operate inside that framework's blind spots.

Many of the supply chain controls embedded in today's regulatory frameworks are artifacts of an earlier era. Some date back to the early 2000s, when concerns about supplier integrity focused more on contract compliance and business continuity than on code provenance or embedded threat vectors. At that time, supply chain risk was framed around vendor reliability —not adversarial infiltration. The assumptions were different. The threat model was incomplete. And in many frameworks, the language hasn't caught up.

Why? Because regulatory frameworks—particularly in critical infrastructure—are not unilaterally imposed. They are often the result of prolonged negotiation between regulators and industry stakeholders. Every control, every requirement, every expectation must be discussed, justified, and aligned with operational realities. Updates require consensus, and consensus is difficult when the changes imply significant retooling, increased transparency, or disruption to long-standing vendor relationships.

Modernizing supply chain controls would mean asking hard questions that many organizations aren't ready to answer. It would mean demanding software bills of materials (SBOMs) for systems that have never been audited at the firmware level. It would mean requiring vendors to disclose development practices, third-party code inheritances, and build system dependencies. It would mean pushing for memory safety, secure boot, tamper detection—not as enhancements, but as baseline expectations. And for many vendors, that would mean either overhauling their product or conceding that they don't actually know what's inside it.

The result is stasis. Even as the threat landscape has shifted dramatically—from opportunistic exploits to strategic supply chain subversion—many regulatory controls remain frozen in time. What was once a reasonable safeguard now serves as a symbolic gesture: require the vendor to provide a security whitepaper; verify they have a policy. But today's adversaries don't care about policies. They target the CI/CD pipeline. They intercept driver updates. They compromise developers.

And so, the frameworks remain out of step. Not because

regulators don't understand the risk—but because changing the rules requires changing the ecosystem. And that is a political, economic, and operational challenge that exceeds the scope of any single audit cycle.

Worse still, exceptions—once approved—often become entrenched. An unpatched system is given a temporary waiver because it's "too critical to take down." A legacy PLC is allowed to use plaintext protocols because encryption isn't supported. A vendor is granted direct VPN access for maintenance. These exceptions are all documented, justified, and signed off. But they're rarely revisited. Over time, they become invisible —accepted risks that quietly undermine the architecture of control they were once meant to preserve.

The illusion of security extends into incident response. When a breach occurs in a compliant environment, defenders often waste precious time chasing documented controls that don't actually work. They assume segmentation exists because it's in the diagram. They believe logging is functional because the policy says it should be. They expect MFA to be enabled because the spreadsheet lists it. These assumptions delay detection and misguide response—because the ground truth differs from the compliance reality.

There's also a psychological toll. Once a control is deemed compliant, it becomes institutionalized. Engineers are discouraged from changing approved designs. Analysts hesitate to challenge assumptions. Security teams develop what could be called "green box fatigue"—a resistance to revisiting controls that have already passed inspection. In this way, compliance becomes not just a static posture, but a cognitive barrier to improvement. Curiosity is dulled. Questioning is discouraged. The illusion is defended more fiercely than the infrastructure it claims to protect.

In the nuclear sector, cybersecurity isn't limited to reviewing diagrams or watching logs—it's a discipline grounded in physical verification. At many nuclear power plants, cybersecurity teams conduct regular walkdowns of the actual control environment. These are not abstract reviews—they are hands-on inspections. The teams trace wiring, confirm conduit runs, inspect HMIs, PLCs, and network switches, and verify that unused ports are secured or disabled. They check patch panels, search for unauthorized equipment, validate lockout points, and confirm that every asset listed in the documentation exists, is connected as expected, and hasn't drifted from the approved configuration.

Just as critically, they use these walkdowns to validate that controls are not only present, but functional, and documented accurately. If a policy requires physical port blocking, the walkdown confirms it's implemented. If segmentation is defined in the network diagram, the walkdown confirms there's no crossover. If a diode is in place, they validate that no bypass exists. Each control is reviewed in the real world, not just on paper—and if a control doesn't function as intended, or isn't aligned with how it's described, it is recorded and corrected, not excused.

This operational discipline is a core reason why nuclear cybersecurity programs remain among the most mature in critical infrastructure. They understand that in a system as complex and risk-sensitive as a nuclear plant, you don't trust what's documented—you verify what's real.

That mindset has broad applicability. In manufacturing plants, water systems, chemical facilities, and refineries, similar walkdowns could reveal hidden risks—legacy switches wired into critical paths, misused USB charging ports, undocumented patch cables, maintenance laptops plugged into control segments, or segmentation boundaries that don't hold. None of these would show up in a policy review. But all of them could become points of compromise.

Walkdowns bring visibility to the gray areas—between

intention and execution, between policy and implementation, between what is assumed and what actually exists. They expose drift. They correct myth. And most importantly, they turn security from a documentation exercise into a firsthand operational truth.

Cybersecurity isn't a checklist—it's a conversation. Every control that exists is, or should be, the answer to a question. If you implement MFA, it's not because a framework told you to—it's because you asked, "What if someone steals a password?" If you isolate your OT network from enterprise systems, it's not because a standard mandates it—it's because you asked, "What happens if accounting gets phished?"

In this way, every line of your architecture becomes a response to an imagined scenario. Every safeguard is the artifact of curiosity. Every control is an answer.

The mistake many organizations make is in skipping the question. They implement the control without understanding what it's supposed to prevent. And over time, they forget what the question was in the first place. The control becomes an obligation instead of an insight.

But when you build with a questioning attitude, the control becomes meaningful again. It reflects thought. It reflects risk awareness. It reflects an active engagement with the complexity of the environment. And when the environment changes—as it always does—you're more likely to ask the question again, rather than blindly trust the old answer.

This is what separates real cybersecurity from paper shields. A compliant system is one where the boxes are checked. A secure system is one where the questions are still being asked.

Because when the adversary comes—and they will—they won't care about your audit trail. They'll care about your reality. And they will not be stopped by a paper shield.

CHAPTER 34 - THE PATH FORWARD: COEXISTENCE, COMPENSATION, OR COLLAPSE

There is a certain gravity to legacy. In the world of industrial control systems, where uptime is sacred and change is measured in decades, legacy protocols are not mere artifacts of the past—they are active participants in the present. They issue commands to turbines, monitor tank levels, switch breakers, and log sensor readings. They do their jobs quietly, efficiently, and without fanfare. But they were never built to do that job in a world at war.

This book has made the case, in technical detail and historical context, that many of the protocols underpinning industrial operations today are fundamentally insecure. They were designed for deterministic timing and trusted topologies, not cryptographic resilience or adversarial fault tolerance. They move messages without validation, authenticate nothing, and assume that whoever is speaking is authorized to do so. In the absence of governance, modernization, or replacement, these protocols are now colliding with a threat landscape that has learned to weaponize their design.

So the question becomes: what now?

The path forward is not singular. It cannot be. The industrial world is too complex, too diverse, and too economically constrained for a one-size-fits-all solution. What emerges instead are three broad strategic approaches—coexistence, compensation, and collapse prevention. Each reflects a different philosophy of risk management. Each imposes its own costs, its own tradeoffs, its own trajectory. But all begin with the same premise: we cannot secure what we do not understand, and we cannot modernize what we are unwilling to admit is broken.

The first path—coexistence—accepts that insecure protocols will remain in place for the foreseeable future. It is the most common strategy by necessity. Full protocol replacement is impractical for many environments. The devices are too old, the budgets too limited, the downtime too expensive. Instead, insecure protocols are isolated, monitored, and shielded from abuse through architectural controls. Firewalls segment traffic. Data diodes enforce one-way flows. Intrusion detection systems watch for anomalies in Modbus or BACnet commands. Access to engineering workstations is hardened. Out-of-band channels are restricted. Risk is not eliminated—it is contained.

This model is deeply familiar to operators. It reflects how they've always managed mechanical failure or human error: anticipate, contain, recover. But coexistence demands constant vigilance. It assumes that the insecure protocol is never directly exposed to the threat. And that assumption must be maintained with unrelenting discipline. Once segmentation is misconfigured, or monitoring is bypassed, or a rogue actor gains access to a trusted zone, the insecure protocol becomes a liability once again. The success of this strategy depends on an operator's ability to maintain strict boundaries—not just on a network diagram, but in practice, under pressure, at scale.

The second path—compensation—treats insecure protocols as immutable and wraps them in layers of security. In this model, legacy is neither replaced nor quarantined. It is augmented. Gateway devices convert insecure traffic into secure messages. Application-layer proxies enforce policy before commands are allowed to pass. Digital twins simulate protocol behavior in safe testbeds. Behavioral analytics build profiles of expected function and raise alerts on deviations. In some cases, TLS tunnels or VPN overlays encapsulate insecure payloads, preserving determinism while adding confidentiality and authentication at the transport layer.

This approach is attractive because it promises security without disruption. It allows operators to extend the life of installed systems while reducing exposure to attack. But compensation has limits. It requires deep understanding of protocol behavior, careful integration of compensating controls, and acceptance of false positives in behavioral detection. It also depends on tools and vendors that may not be fully aligned with the operational lifecycle of critical infrastructure. A security shim that is unsupported in three years offers little value in a system designed to last thirty. Compensation is not a permanent solution. It is a strategy of buying time—and using that time wisely.

The third path—collapse prevention through phased replacement—is the most aggressive, the most expensive, and ultimately, the most necessary. This strategy begins by acknowledging that some protocols must be removed from the ecosystem entirely. No amount of segmentation or shielding will make unauthenticated, plaintext control messages safe in a world where state-backed attackers know how to exploit them. Protocols that lack even the capacity for cryptographic identity or session integrity cannot be allowed to persist in critical functions forever.

Phased replacement is not about ripping and replacing every RTU or sensor overnight. It is about setting timelines, allocating budget, and aligning vendors to a shared roadmap. It requires operators to categorize systems by risk, identify the most dangerous protocol exposures, and prioritize upgrades accordingly. It also demands vendor cooperation—products that support secure protocol variants, documentation that facilitates migration, and APIs that allow for interoperability during the transition period. It is not quick. It is not cheap. But it is the only strategy that moves the industry toward a future in which protocol trust is native, not layered on top.

To guide these decisions, defenders might begin to think in terms of a protocol lifecycle—five informal stages that map technical risk to organizational urgency. Introduction represents new protocols designed with security in mind. Adoption includes early use with inconsistent enforcement. Dependence is where most ICS protocols live today: widely used, poorly secured, and difficult to replace. Inertia sets in when patching slows and migration plans stall. Finally, Obsolescence defines protocols that cannot be secured and must be scheduled for removal. Mapping where a system sits in this lifecycle offers a more realistic way to assign both urgency and budget.

Many organizations will pursue all three strategies—coexistence, compensation, replacement—in parallel. They will isolate what they must, compensate where they can, and replace where they have the opportunity. What matters is not ideological purity, but clarity of purpose. Each insecure protocol still in use must have a defined strategy: containment, compensation, or retirement. Undefined risk is unmanaged risk. And unmanaged risk is what adversaries exploit.

Some industries are already moving. The electric sector, nudged by NERC CIP requirements, has invested in segmentation and protocol monitoring. The water sector, prompted by headline breaches and government scrutiny, is reevaluating remote access and unauthenticated control pathways. Oil and gas operators, facing the combined pressure of ransomware and regulatory exposure, are beginning to integrate protocol-level risk into procurement. None of these changes are complete. But they are real.

Still, inertia remains powerful. And among the frontline defenders—the engineers and security professionals who hold the line between fragile systems and real-world consequences

—there is fatigue. A technician in a municipal water plant has patched the same vulnerable field device four times in two years. The alerts don't stop. The tools aren't made for her environment. And the risk, like the protocol, never seems to go away. Responsibility without authority wears people down. Governance, if it is to be meaningful, must include the human systems who carry the operational burden every day.

Nor does collapse have to come from the center. The weakest link is often not the core RTU or the PLC in a protected cabinet —but the third-party wireless sensor added for convenience, or the aging remote terminal forgotten in a maintenance shed. These devices come into the ecosystem through supply chains that are not always vetted, using default configurations that are rarely updated, running firmware no one can inspect. Collapse often begins not with a bang, but with a cracked hinge. And when protocols cannot be trusted, supply chains must be treated as contested space.

All the while, the adversary advances. Attackers don't need to support legacy systems. They don't worry about vendor interoperability or recertification delays. They exploit what exists. They write flexible tools and evolve quickly. They don't face procurement committees. They don't wait for industry consortia to agree on terminology. The asymmetry is stark: defenders are bound by process, while adversaries are bound only by imagination. That is why delay is dangerous. The adversary doesn't need to modernize an entire fleet. They need only find the one device still speaking 1997. In that asymmetry lies the urgency to act.

And yet, defenders face another risk: knowledge loss. Many systems persist not because they are robust, but because the few people who understood them never documented their work. As those engineers retire or move on, institutional memory fades. Protocol behavior becomes folklore. And with it, the ability to safely manage or modernize vanishes. Some systems remain untouched not because they are secure—but because no one alive remembers how they were built.

Global coordination is needed now more than ever—but even that is showing signs of fracture. While some countries are pushing for interoperable, secure standards across the ICS landscape, others are drifting toward proprietary stacks, domestic-only ecosystems, and tightly controlled industrial protocols that may not conform to global norms. If this fragmentation continues, we may face a future where protocols are not just insecure, but incompatible—turning the global industrial base into an archipelago of siloed risk, ungovernable at scale.

But this story does not need to end in collapse. It can end in transformation.

Imagine a future not far from now. An engineer connects to a system for routine maintenance. Before a single message is exchanged, the endpoint verifies its firmware signature and authenticates its identity using a cryptographic trust anchor. The network policy enforcer checks that the protocol being used conforms to an approved secure profile. If it doesn't, the connection is refused. A dashboard flags a legacy device nearing end-of-life, not with a vague risk score, but with a clear decommission date, a tested migration path, and vendor-supported tooling. Security isn't layered on—it's embedded. Trusted communication is the norm, not the exception.

That future is possible. It's not utopian. It's just disciplined.

We know what this takes. It takes procurement language that prioritizes protocol security. It takes regulators willing to demand minimum standards. It takes vendors who commit to sunset insecure modes and support migration paths. It takes certification bodies who test for security as rigorously as they test for function. It takes system integrators who treat protocols not just as compatibility layers, but as the fabric of trust. And it takes leadership willing to say: this is no longer acceptable.

Most importantly, it takes collaboration across every layer of the industrial stack. This is not a vendor problem. It is not a plant-floor problem. It is not a government problem. It is all of them. Protocol insecurity will not be resolved by any single role acting alone. Engineers, cybersecurity teams, product designers, integrators, auditors, regulators, and operators must act from the same threat model, guided by the same principles: visibility, authenticity, and control.

Because protocols are not just wires and packets. They are governance in code. They are trust expressed in timing, in syntax, in assumed identity. And in a world where trust is under siege, they must evolve.

The path forward will not be smooth. But it can be navigated. With clear governance, realistic timelines, investment in tooling, and alignment between security and engineering, the industry can adapt. Protocols will not be fixed overnight. Some may never be fixed. But coexistence, compensation, and replacement offer a way forward—a strategy for managing what we inherited until we can build what we need.

Because the alternative is collapse. And we've seen what that looks like.

We still have time. But not forever. The path forward is narrow, but it exists.

And now, more than ever, it must be taken.

CHAPTER 35 - THE FUTURE OF PROTOCOL GOVERNANCE AND STANDARDIZATION

For all the technical scrutiny heaped upon industrial protocols —the buffer overflows, the cleartext transmissions, the unauthenticated writes—less is said about how these protocols came to be what they are. Their weaknesses are not just technical artifacts; they are symptoms of a deeper problem: the absence of centralized, cohesive governance. In contrast to the tight, formal ecosystems that govern internet protocols or enterprise cryptography, the industrial space is fragmented, with overlapping consortia, proprietary interests, and legacy inertia pulling protocol evolution in divergent directions. What results is not merely a patchwork of designs, but a labyrinth of competing interests and half-finished standards that too often leave security as an afterthought.

Unlike the Internet Engineering Task Force (IETF) or the World Wide Web Consortium (W3C), which operate through open participation and well-defined processes, industrial protocol development has historically been dominated by vendors. A protocol might originate inside a single company—Modbus from Modicon, CIP from Allen-Bradley, DNP3 from GE and Westronic—and only later be handed off to standards organizations for broader stewardship. Even then, the handoff is rarely clean. Multiple variants proliferate, proprietary extensions muddy the water, and implementation guidance is often either sparse or riddled with loopholes. As a result, the same protocol can behave differently depending on whose devices are talking. Compliance becomes a matter of interpretation, not a guarantee of interoperability or security.

This fractured development history has had lasting consequences. In many industrial settings, protocol selection is less about technical merit and more about historical accident. A facility built around Siemens equipment in the 1990s will likely still be speaking PROFINET or PROFIBUS today—not because those protocols offer superior security, but because replacing them would be prohibitively expensive and disruptive. These are not transient decisions. They calcify. And because industrial systems are expected to last for decades, insecure deployments have a long tail. Devices running twenty-year-old firmware still control substations, water pumps, and manufacturing lines. Updating them isn't always an option. For many operators, the cost of downtime dwarfs the abstract risk of a cyberattack. The result is a persistent ecosystem of unpatchable, unreplaceable, and often invisible protocol-level vulnerabilities.

Complicating matters further is the global asymmetry in protocol modernization. While North American, European, and East Asian critical infrastructure operators increasingly fold protocol security into their broader risk posture, the same cannot always be said for developing regions. Economic constraints, lack of regulatory pressure, and limited access to secure alternatives leave many facilities relying on legacy systems with no real path forward. In a small South American water treatment facility, for instance, a series of legacy PLCs operating over Modbus/TCP remained exposed for years due to budget restrictions and an inability to integrate newer protocol stacks. Eventually, the facility became the target of a foreign actor who used that exposure as a pivot point—less for sabotage than for testing a foothold in a transnational infrastructure chain. The attack never made headlines, but it underscored a reality the industry often ignores: insecure protocols don't just expose a local system—they expose everyone connected downstream.

Yet for all the calls for modernization, any serious conversation about protocol governance must confront a fundamental constraint: the enduring weight of backward compatibility. In the OT world, this is not a feature—it's a necessity. Entire industrial systems run on devices that are either too old to update, too costly to replace, or locked into regulatory certification regimes that prohibit even minor changes. Many of these devices have no file system, no secure boot process, no update mechanism whatsoever. They were designed for deterministic control in isolated environments, not cryptographic negotiation over converged networks. In some cases, even trying to update them would void safety certifications or trigger cascading recertification cycles.

This presents a governance dilemma. If protocol security depends on devices being upgradeable, and many devices simply aren't, what then? The answer is layered containment. Rather than trying to retrofit encryption and authentication into every endpoint, the focus must shift to compensating architectural controls—network segmentation, protocol-aware firewalls, unidirectional gateways, and anomaly detection that wraps insecure protocols in protective monitoring. It's not a perfect solution. But it buys time and reduces risk in environments where the alternative is doing nothing at all.

Some industry groups have begun to acknowledge this layered reality. The ISA/IEC 62443 framework, for example, explicitly recognizes that legacy devices may lack native security capabilities and recommends architectural segmentation as a compensating safeguard. Likewise, the U.S. Department of Energy's Cyber-Informed Engineering initiative emphasizes risk-informed design, where insecure protocols are accounted for in the broader context of system resilience. But these approaches work best when there is visibility—and that's often lacking. Many operators don't even know which protocols are in use across their environments, or which devices are capable of being upgraded. Governance must begin with inventory.

Ultimately, backward compatibility cannot be treated as an excuse for inaction, nor as an immutable law. Instead, it must be managed as a constraint—one that shapes the cadence and scope of modernization. Protocol governance must differentiate between three categories of systems: those that can be upgraded, those that can be mitigated, and those that must eventually be retired. This triage model allows for realistic prioritization. It recognizes that protocol security is not just about writing secure code—it's about managing the inertia of infrastructure built on insecure foundations.

Vendors, too, must take a more active role in managing backward compatibility. That means providing clearly documented end-of-life timelines, offering protocol shims that allow legacy devices to speak through secure gateways, and designing future products with long-term update paths. In many cases, protocol wrappers or proxy architectures can allow older devices to participate in secure communication sessions without internal change. These solutions are not ideal, but they represent a bridge between the insecure past and the more resilient future.

Governance efforts must also grapple with a broader systemic flaw: the lack of economic accountability for insecure protocols. The costs of failure—operational downtime, regulatory fines, or physical damage—are borne by the asset owner. But the vendor who shipped the protocol stack often has no liability. In practice, this has created an ecosystem where risk is externalized. There is no financial penalty for insecure default behavior, no breach-triggered recourse that compels vendors to modernize their offerings. Until procurement contracts, regulations, or litigation frameworks create consequences for poor protocol hygiene, the economic incentive to modernize will lag behind the technical need. It was only under liability and safety mandates that industries like automotive and aviation evolved from best practices to baseline requirements. Industrial cybersecurity is on that same trajectory—still early, but accelerating.

Some forward-leaning organizations are addressing modernization challenges with modeling tools. One promising strategy involves digital twins—virtual representations of physical OT environments. By simulating protocol interactions and device behavior under load, digital twins allow operators to test secure protocol migration scenarios in a sandboxed environment. At a major European utility, engineers used a digital twin of their SCADA and substation control infrastructure to model the migration from DNP3 to Secure DNP3. This allowed them to identify compatibility issues, tune latency-sensitive parameters, and build a rollout plan grounded in data rather than assumptions. Digital twins are not only planning tools—they are governance accelerators.

The modernization of protocols also intersects with a more profound shift in control logic itself: autonomy. As machine learning systems are introduced into OT environments— to manage load balancing, energy optimization, anomaly detection, and predictive maintenance—the trustworthiness of data takes on new urgency. Protocols that transmit control commands and state data become not just vectors of function, but anchors of machine decision-making. A spoofed message may not raise an alarm if it conforms to expected structure—but it may influence an ML model to take actions that no human ever sees. The more automated the system, the higher the stakes of protocol integrity. As AI assumes a larger role in OT operations, protocol trust must move from optional to foundational.

Regulatory pressure has begun to shift this landscape, albeit unevenly. In the United States, organizations like NERC and FERC have issued guidelines and requirements for critical infrastructure, while the Department of Homeland Security has worked through CISA to publish best practices and sector-specific guidance. In Europe, the NIS Directive and associated ENISA frameworks provide a similar push toward improving cybersecurity hygiene across essential services. In

Germany, the IT-Sicherheitsgesetz introduced direct obligations for infrastructure providers, catalyzing collaboration among operators, vendors, and government agencies. These interventions rarely mandate specific protocols, but they have created a culture of risk awareness and change. In some cases, regulation has become the catalyst for long-delayed modernization. In others, it has sparked necessary conversations, even where implementation lags.

Some of the most promising signs of forward momentum have come from the open source community. Projects such as *open62541* for OPC UA, *libmodbus* for Modbus, and *pycomm3* for Ethernet/IP have made it possible for researchers, integrators, and defenders to study and validate industrial protocol behavior at scale. These tools lower the barrier for experimentation, fuzzing, and custom security enforcement layers. Open source ecosystems also bring transparency to implementation, which is critical for trust-building in an environment long defined by black boxes. In many cases, the security tooling used to detect and mitigate protocol vulnerabilities is built and maintained by independent researchers and non-profit groups—filling a void left by vendor reticence and limited commercial incentives.

Just as important are the advances in behavioral analytics applied to protocol traffic. In the absence of secure design, some defenders have turned to passive inspection and machine learning to identify anomalous activity over insecure protocols. Rather than relying on authentication headers or signed messages, these systems develop a profile of expected behavior —frequency, structure, command patterns—and flag deviations that might indicate compromise. These technologies, while not replacements for secure design, offer a powerful layer of compensating control in environments where replacement is not immediately feasible. Over time, such tools can even help inform long-term migration planning by identifying which devices behave most predictably and which pose the greatest risk.

Beyond the technical, there is a growing awareness that governance must evolve from patchwork to global coordination. Just as the maritime, nuclear, and aviation industries have established international conventions for safety and reliability, the industrial cybersecurity domain may soon need an equivalent. What would it look like for nations to agree on a global baseline for protocol behavior in critical infrastructure? Such a framework would not dictate every implementation detail, but it could establish minimum criteria for authentication, encryption, session integrity, and protocol transparency. It could define sunset timelines for high-risk protocol features, similar to how encryption standards are phased out over time. While no such framework exists today, its necessity grows clearer with every new attack that crosses borders.

And yet, technical and regulatory challenges are only part of the story. Cultural and organizational inertia remains one of the most intractable barriers to protocol governance. In many enterprises, responsibility for protocols falls into a crack between departments. The cybersecurity team may be responsible for network security but has no authority over industrial protocol selection. The control engineers, meanwhile, are deeply familiar with system behavior but may have little training or incentive to prioritize security. Governance doesn't fail only at the standards table—it fails in the day-to-day decisions where no one owns the protocol risk. Until organizations designate clear ownership for protocol security—and align incentives, training, and decision-making accordingly—even the best standards will remain under-implemented.

There's a human story buried in this, too. Somewhere in the middle of America, or Europe, or Asia, a control systems engineer has just received a memo from a vendor: a new firmware update will enforce TLS communication, breaking backward compatibility with a fleet of old SCADA software. She has no budget for upgrades, no staffing to retest the system, and no mandate from management to force a change. The secure path is technically available—but economically and organizationally out of reach. That's the real-world edge of protocol governance: the place where theory meets constraint. Until governance accounts for those constraints—and offers support, timelines, and shared tools—the promise of secure protocols will remain, for many, just out of reach.

Protocol security in the industrial domain will not be achieved by technical fixes alone. It requires governance. It requires leadership. And it requires a willingness to confront the uncomfortable reality that many of today's systems are built atop foundations that were never designed to bear the weight of an adversarial world. The question now is whether we continue to accept that—or whether we begin, finally, to build something better.

CHAPTER 36 – CONVERGENCE: SECURING OUR LEGACY, SHAPING OUR FUTURE

In the pages preceding this final chapter, we've traced the evolution of operational technology—from the early days when air gaps and isolated networks equated to safety, to today's interconnected environments where legacy OT/ICS systems remain central to critical infrastructure. Our journey has honored both the enduring resilience of systems designed to last decades and the urgent challenges posed by modern cyber threats. Now, standing at the final convergence of past experience and future innovation, we are reminded that our mission is not defined by a single victory or failure, but by an ongoing commitment to safeguarding the operational core of industry.

Throughout this book, we have seen that legacy systems—once praised for their reliability and deterministic operation—are not relics to be discarded, but foundations upon which modern security must be constructed. The transition from isolated architectures to complex, integrated networks has revealed vulnerabilities that demand a layered, defense-in-depth strategy. We explored the painstaking process of retrofitting aging systems with contemporary safeguards: managing patches in environments that can't afford downtime, offloading security functions to external modules to preserve system resources, and introducing encryption and real-time monitoring without jeopardizing the deterministic timing essential to industrial operations.

But technical challenges are only half the battle. A recurring theme has been the human factor—the cultural chasm that persists between IT and OT disciplines. In traditional industrial contexts, engineers relied on physical segregation and tightly scoped devices. Today, however, the merging of digital and physical realms requires new norms of collaboration. Cross-disciplinary teams must come together to build solutions that are both resilient and operationally sustainable. Training programs, ongoing dialogue, and the development of a shared technical vocabulary are not just enablers—they are prerequisites for resilience.

Risk management has emerged as a central pillar. Unlike the binary mindset of earlier eras, modern OT cybersecurity requires a nuanced view—one that acknowledges that a single rare event can still yield catastrophic consequences. We've moved beyond static checklists toward dynamic, evolving assessments that consider probability, impact, and consequence across multiple timeframes. Organizations have begun to shift from viewing compliance as a destination to treating it as a baseline, recalibrating their posture in light of real-world complexity, evolving threats, and changing operational priorities.

Regulatory frameworks and standards have also played a defining role. In navigating the landscape of NERC CIP, NIST CSF, IEC 62443, and other mandates, we came to understand that regulatory compliance should be viewed as a floor, not a ceiling. These frameworks have prompted organizations to adopt more mature cybersecurity practices, not just to meet legal obligations but to protect reputations, ensure safety, and future-proof operations. In this light, regulation becomes a catalyst—not a constraint—for innovation, pushing security into the core of business decisions, procurement cycles, training efforts, and organizational culture.

Looking ahead, the future of OT/ICS cybersecurity is filled with both uncertainty and opportunity. Technologies such as artificial intelligence, machine learning, and digital twin simulation offer new ways to anticipate and mitigate risks. These tools could help us shift from reactive defense to predictive, adaptive protection—enabling us to model the effects of vulnerabilities before they are exploited and continuously adjust our posture as threats evolve. But these gains must not come at the expense of operational stability. As we adopt new technologies, we must also retain the precision, safety, and predictability that industrial environments require.

This final chapter is more than a conclusion—it is a call to action. The convergence of legacy resilience with modern ingenuity is not an endpoint, but a continuous journey. Every innovation, every collaborative breakthrough, and every small improvement strengthens the fabric of our defenses. While adversaries need only succeed once, defenders must be vigilant every time. This is the essence of defense-in-depth: layers of protection working in concert to ensure that even if one barrier fails, others stand ready to preserve safety and continuity.

When we step back and synthesize the lessons across this book, a central truth emerges: the way forward does not lie in rejecting the past but in integrating it wisely. Legacy systems do not just represent technical debt; they embody decades of operational insight, process knowledge, and hard-won reliability. When this experience is married to modern security frameworks, the result is a hybrid approach—one that blends institutional memory with adaptive innovation.

As we close, let us acknowledge that the path ahead is neither easy nor guaranteed. But the future of OT cybersecurity is not written in code alone. It is shaped by people—by their decisions, their vigilance, and their commitment to excellence. Building secure industrial systems is not a one-time project. It is a process of relentless refinement, continuous learning, and principled resilience. When we integrate legacy and modern systems with thoughtfulness and rigor, we do more than preserve operations —we create a platform for innovation, a safe harbor for progress, and a model for what cybersecurity can become in an age of convergence.

This book is a chronicle of that journey. Whether you are an engineer safeguarding control systems, a CISO designing policy, or a technician maintaining PLCs on the plant floor, know that your work matters. The legacy we inherit is not an anchor—it is a launching point. It is our responsibility to build forward, with creativity and precision, toward a more secure, intelligent, and sustainable industrial future.

The final convergence is not the end. It is the beginning of a partnership—between past and future, between reliability and innovation, between the physical and the digital. May this work inspire you to continue that journey, defend what matters most, and shape the secure systems that tomorrow will depend on.

ABOUT THE AUTHOR

Bill Johns began his journey into the world of computing over 45 years ago, starting as a hobbyist building and upgrading computer hardware. His natural curiosity and technical aptitude soon led him to explore computer networks, and before long, he had built a large Bulletin Board System (BBS) that became a hub for early online communities. At the same time, Bill was applying his growing expertise to building corporate networks, helping businesses navigate the new landscape of interconnected systems.

When the internet began to take shape, Bill adapted his BBS to the online world, delving deep into internet protocols by reading RFCs (Request for Comments) and engaging with fellow tech pioneers on the Undernet, Dalnet, EfNet, and similar forums. His deep understanding of networks and security caught the attention of a major social networking platform, where motivated by relentless attacks, he gained admin privileges on the network's servers through sheer skill and ingenuity. Faced with an ultimatum — explain how he did it and use his knowledge to defend the network, or face the consequences — Bill chose the high road. This decision launched him into several intense years of 24/7 live-fire hacker wars, where he was on the front lines defending critical systems from relentless attacks.

This battle-hardened experience opened the door to high-stakes contracts, including responding to the devastating effects of malware like Code Red and Nimda. Bill was brought in to help recover paralyzed networks that had been written off as lost causes — and he succeeded where others had failed. Once the dust settled from the early 2000s malware wars, Bill shifted his focus to building secure networks for U.S. Department of Defense (DoD) contractors, helping to protect national security infrastructure from emerging cyber threats.

Later in his career, Bill turned his expertise toward securing critical infrastructure, including IT and OT/ICS environments. His work spanned industries such as manufacturing, oil and gas, pharmaceuticals, automotive, water and wastewater systems, electrical power generation, and nuclear power plants. Bill's accumulated knowledge and experience, stretching back to the early days of computer networking and the internet, provide a rare and invaluable perspective on the evolution of cybersecurity. His books reflect the hard-won lessons and insights gained from a career spent not just observing but actively shaping the development of secure digital systems.

www.ingramcontent.com/pod-product-compliance
Lightning Source LLC
LaVergne TN
LVHW051440050326
832903LV00030BD/3176